The Poet

The
Poetry of Chess

edited and introduced by
Andrew Waterman

Anvil Press Poetry

Published in 1981
by Anvil Press Poetry Ltd
69 King George Street London SE10 8PX
Distributed by Wildwood House Ltd
ISBN 0 85646 067 2

This book is published
with financial assistance from
the Arts Council of Great Britain

Printed and bound in Great Britain at
The Camelot Press Ltd, Southampton

Contents

2 Players

3 Philosophies

4 Moralities

5 Public Worlds

6 Personal Relations

Introduction

My aim in *The Poetry of Chess* has been to collect good poetry in English of any period or provenance that uses chess and chess concepts figuratively to express human themes, together with a few poems about the game itself. I have included translations only in a few cases, such as Fitzgerald's *Rubáiyát*, Goldsmith's version of Vida or Lowell's of Montale, where these effectively have standing as English-language poetry. That such an anthology lacks predecessors, for the few previous compilations of 'literary' material about chess draw cursorily upon poetry compared with prose fiction and other writing, is perhaps surprising. Chess has been around a long time. Established in north-west India by the sixth century, within a few hundred years it became, by courtesy of Moorish invasions and the cultural imperialism of those travelling people the Vikings – enthusiastic players in lulls between their more nefarious activities – a familiar pastime throughout the European nobility. The nature of the game, its microcosmic chequer-board approximation to war, or to aspects of the human condition in a universe moved by mysterious forces, its version of a status-bound society in which, however, the merest pawn may win promotion, or checkmate as well as die for a king; its conclusion in royal death, and the return of all pieces to a wooden box; and the virtually infinite variety of possible positions and choices of moves during play, every blunder haunted by neglected alternatives: such things have made chess over the centuries a rich source of suggestive metaphor for man's thoughts about himself and his society, his relationship to God or fate, or to other people. Poets have noticed this. My hope is that both poetry-readers and chess players will find pleasure in a collection of poems widely diverse, except for the chess connection, in kind and in human themes. Although a few have claimed inclusion as interesting curiosities, poetic merit has been the main criterion in choosing from the material available: chess, like love, is not unburdened with the versifying of those whose literary talent is inadequate to their passion.

'Chess, like love, like music, has the power to make men happy', wrote the great German player and theoretician Siegbert Tarrasch. He might equally have mentioned poetry. The comparison to music of a game satisfying both the intellect and the aesthetic and emotional senses with its abstract articulation of silent harmonies, orchestrated combinations, recurring variable themes and elegant resolutions, has commonly been made. Particular great chess players have been likened stylistically to composers: Capablanca, World Champion from 1921 to 1927, to Mozart; his successor Alekhine to Wagner. Chess also, like mathematics, shares with music not only some innate qualities, but being an area of human endeavour where because mastery does not depend on experience of or reference to any world beyond itself precocious youthful achievement can occur. A writer, his medium words which inescapably denote and mediate things in human experience beyond words, needs to have got a little more living in.

One feature of chess which strikes me as a poet is that with its fusion of intellectual and imaginative faculties the game offers something about as close as one can get to that unquantifiable but recognizable phenomenon essential creativity, utterly divorced from experience of or engagement with life, as in poetry it by definition cannot be, and nourished purely by commitment to chess itself; yet by virtue of that very isolation, and the game's nature, its exponents are subject to intense, potentially warping psychological pressures. All this, in its various aspects, seems worth exploring in some detail.

If chess does not mediate life, it certainly utters the creative temperament of its players. In chess, as in poetry, the style is the man, profoundly expressive of moral as well as artistic and intellectual qualities. Tal's games are as distinguishable from Karpov's as Tennyson's poetry is from Browning's. One might amuse oneself by pairing chess players with poets: Korchnoi with Lowell, both risk-taking complicators, unsettlers of equilibrium who sometimes overreach, temperamentally drawn to dangerous edges to elicit harmony from the chaos of the material; the craggy, combative Lasker, pragmatic yet philosophical, profound yet undecorative, with Wordsworth; Morphy with Marvell, to whom T. S. Eliot attributed 'tough reasonableness beneath the slight lyric grace'; Nimzowitsch, triumphing through the arcane and concocting theory from his highly subjective chess practice, with the early Eliot himself, writing that most idiosyncratically personal poem *The Waste Land* under the auspices of his 'impersonal theory of art'; Petrosian, winning by mystifying ingenuities of non-commitment, is the Samuel Beckett of chess; the baroque opacities of Alekhine recall

Hopkins; the crystalline classical profundities of Capablanca, Pushkin. Like poetry, chess has had its phases of romanticism, classicism, modernism. In the classical period, early this century, opening play at grandmaster level was as unquestionedly dominated by the Queen's Gambit Declined as was poetry's Augustan Age by what it prematurely supposed to be the ultimate refinement of versification, the heroic couplet. At chess tournaments the talk among players and spectators – revolving around such matters as Miles's latest tournament, someone else's 'masterpiece' or 'brilliancy' or *Complete Games*, 'early' as opposed to 'late' Keres, Kasparov's potential, the merits of the d6 wedge in the Leningrad system against the Nimzo, an exchange sacrifice in the Sicilian, this year's fashionable openings, why Korchnoi forsook the French Defence, and so forth – all reminds me strongly of literary discussion among writers and critics: familiar, obsessive, only the terms different, as if one had switched to another language.

Some literary academics might, incidentally, note Capablanca's remarks in *My Chess Career*, drawing attention to

the poor notes sometimes written by analysts. Games are often annotated by unknown players who have not sufficient knowledge of the game. As a matter of fact, the games of the great masters, at least, can only be properly annotated by very few players. Of course even the best are not exempt from mistakes, but while they make them few and far between the others do so continuously.[1]

Wordsworth felt comparably about the critical analysis of poetry. Yet while the moderate chess player, who ought indeed and nowadays in general does refrain, not from studying, but from attempting publishable annotation of grandmaster games, at least has considerable experience of playing chess, armies of academics instead of sticking to their proper tasks of presenting literature to the young and the modest clerical work of routine scholarship, burden libraries with inept literary-critical explication undeterred by their lack of first-hand experience of creative writing.

Turning to the creative process itself, the implementation of creative conceptions, one finds interesting resemblances in accounts given by chess players and poets. Capablanca, referring to his own play, writes of

four games which, although of quite different types, bear certain distinct characteristics which show the hand of the same master: the plans are built on

[1] J. R. Capablanca, *My Chess Career*, New York, 1920.

wide though solid lines, the views are large, and in most cases the combinations, whether long or short, as well as the different manoeuvres, are only the tactical means of carrying out the different strategical plans. The general conception, the highest quality in a chess master, is seen to advantage.

Capablanca was a chess classicist, sceptical of romanticism as self-indulgence. His priorities and values here are impeccably Augustan: substitute the word 'metaphors' for 'combinations', and Capablanca's statement about chess masterpieces becomes an absolutely Johnsonian statement about poetry, desiderating that the parts be subordinate and instrumental to overall design, implicitly hostile to needless ornament and unfettered fancy. In novelistic terms Capablanca is a Jamesian, against gratuitous episodic intensification, however creatively rich. His art concealed art, knowing of course that 'apparently simple moves are in reality of a very complicated nature'. Other chess temperaments differ. The creative dynamism of Tal, conjuring mystical transfigurations through opening himself to vertiginous double-edged complexities and intuitions, is profoundly romantic. Annotating one of his own moves '?!' (original but unsound) Tal refers to the 'delight' occasioned 'when grandmasters take chances and are not merely woodshifting.' After a brilliant winning stroke eight moves later, he adds: 'Without taking chances earlier, such a position would scarcely have been reached.'[2] Tal, or Alekhine, might find their articles of faith in Coleridge writing of 'the shaping spirit of imagination', Shelley's conception of creativity as a lighted coal reddened by the inspirational wind, or Blake insisting that 'all great truths' are particular; to generalize is to be an idiot.' While Blake's salutary half-truth may remind chess players as well as poets that neither triumphs through generalized understanding alone, both need, for achieved creativity, a broader technical knowledge to realize their specific perceptions and vision.

Chess has often been defined as a balance of art, science and combat, with different players according to temperament inclining to particular points of that triangle. At least its fusion of inspiration and ratiocination is shared by poetry. And as behind any finished poem lies a penumbra of notions and images glimpsed or considered, 'roads not taken' that were nevertheless integral to composition and necessary to the finished work's particular realization, so it is in chess. The annotation of chess games, showing how awareness of what might happen

[2] J. Hajtun, *Selected Games of Mikhail Tal*, tr. Robert Ejari, 1961.

modified the moves played, demonstrating beautiful latent themes and variations unrealized in, yet charging, the actual play, offers close analogy to explorations of literary creativity and the study of poets' drafts. Alexander Kotov writes in *Play Like a Grandmaster*: 'All variations may be depicted in the form of a tree of analysis in which the variations and sub-variations are represented by the boughs of a tree.'[3] He is defining the process through which, during play, a chess expert calculates to decide his best next move. But what, at critical moments, can suggest the starting-point for a variation thus meticulously analysed, or flickers enlighteningly within the calculative process itself, may come less from logical judgement than crucially from more mysterious sources best describable as inspiration and vision.

Here one recognizes that in every disparate area of mental creativity the nature of the essential moment and process shows affinity. I once heard an eminent scientist, asked on television about higher creativity in astronomy, cite the chess champion Bobby Fischer talking of a 'flash', a brief momentary vision of what might be conjured from the available situation, followed by the sheer detailed labour, necessary but anticlimactic compared with the moment of gestation, almost resented, to realize the conception in actuality. The experience is recognizable to any real poet. Eliot, in 'The Three Voices of Poetry', writes that the poet

has something germinating in him for which he must find words; but he cannot know what words he wants until he has found the words; he cannot identify this embryo until it has been transformed into an arrangement of the right words in the right order. When you have the words for it, the 'thing' for which the words had to be found has disappeared, replaced by a poem.[4]

Or, if 'moves' rather than 'words', by a game of chess. And, Eliot adds, 'He is going to all that trouble . . . to gain relief from acute discomfort.' The account is transposable, I suspect, into terms appropriate to any area of creativity. Germane also is Eliot's observation that 'poetic originality is largely an original way of assembling the most disparate and unlikely material to make a new whole.' In chess, the 'material' is the extant position on the board grasped at the deepest level of its divergent potential, the 'whole' a conclusively harmonious combination or series of manoeuvres elicited from that material.

[3] Alexander Kotov, *Play Like a Grandmaster*, tr. Bernard Cafferty, 1978.
[4] T. S. Eliot, 'The Three Voices of Poetry' (1953), reprinted in *On Poetry and Poets*, 1957.

But here arises the first crucial distinction that divides chess from poetry or other arts. The final criterion of successful chess is victory. In poetry the aesthetic impulse may finally serve a larger moral vision; in chess it attends a purpose more sharply alien. While some players are prone to indulge an aesthetic notion – for example, an attractive but unsound sacrificial combination – in preference to the strongest move, the consequences are more conclusively dire in chess terms than are those of an over-indulged image to a poem. The innate logic of chess as an activity, except in its offshoot mutations the problem and study, inexorably subordinates beauty to the primary practical purpose of winning a game (or title, or tournament). It is a sport ruthless as tennis, its object to inflict defeat. Chess players are notoriously graceless losers, and the end of victory justifies any legal means, and often occasions psychological tricks of gamesmanship. Contrastingly, in poetry the concepts of victory, championship, outscoring the opposition, are meaningless except at the irrelevant level of literary gossip and faction-fighting; true poets are uninterested in the concept of a 'winning' poem, but glad of any real poems they can write. Nor could any equivalent to the expedient 'grandmaster draw', which gains a convenient half-point without risk of loss, have any poetic value whatsoever. And while a poet's enterprise certainly includes struggle, both with his medium and in the sense Frost meant when writing of his 'lover's quarrel with the world', he is spared competitive-collaborative dialectic with an opposing 'player' whose moves must modify his own.

But the most fundamental division between chess and poetry as human activities is suggested by a distinction Wordsworth made in his Preface to *Lyrical Ballads*:

The knowledge both of the Poet and the Man of Science is pleasure; but the knowledge of the one cleaves to us as a necessary part of our existence, our natural and unalienable inheritance; the other is a personal and individual acquisition, slow to come to us, and by no habitual and direct sympathy connecting us with our fellow-beings.[5]

The complexities of chess are much vaster than casual players are likely to realize. In his book ruminating on the extraordinary 1972 Fischer–Spassky World Championship match, the literary polymath George Steiner explains:

Something of the full horror and harmony of the abysmal depths, of the magic

[5] William Wordsworth, *Lyrical Ballads*, Preface to 1802 edition.

of chess vertigo, can be explained numerically. . . . The number of possible ways of playing the first ten moves on each side is such that if every man, woman and child on the earth played without respite it would require more than two hundred and seventeen billion years to go through them all. The most recent estimate of the number of different games that can be played is of the order of 25×10^{115}, a product fantastically larger than the generally assumed sum of atoms in the universe.[6]

No computer can cope with calculation on this scale. Ideally fusing analytical and imaginative faculties, chess has been used in research into the capacity of computers to match the human brain; the results are good news for the latter. Since, despite a computer's amazing rapidity of pure calculation, one cannot hang around for some inordinately galactic length of time while a machine informed merely of the game's rules and object tries to compute White's best opening, programmers have to limit the computer's options, so that apparently senseless moves are not considered, and its move-depth of calculation. Sophisticated methods have been developed for programming computers with positional judgement in chess, and means of evaluating and, according to the position, determining priorities among such various objectives intermediate to ultimate victory as attacking a castled king, material gain, material sacrifice for positional compensation, obtaining a passed pawn that might queen in the endgame. But the best human players, far slower at computation as such, but possessing intuitive positional judgement and sense of pattern, continue to prevail against computer programmes. The human mind's most vital faculties cannot, it seems, be mechanically replicated.

Yet what is all this exercise of what is on occasion genius-level ability humanly for? Playing chess, merely. Almost inexhaustibly profound, chess is also an activity trivial and barren in being wholly self-contained and leading to nothing beyond itself. In the terms of Wordsworth's distinction, it is most extremely 'a personal and individual acquisition' rather than 'a necessary part of our existence'. And if the pure sciences are also in that sense optional human enterprises, not in themselves engaging with the problems of identity, emotion, morality and relationship we all unavoidably experience simply through being human, they have an obvious validity as such in enlarging our understanding of the physical universe which is the conditioning context for our humanity. Chess is wholly sterile. Its play and

[6] George Steiner, *The Sporting Scene: White Knights of Reykjavik*, 1973.

pieces may supply symbols and metaphors for life; the way in which moves and combinations *not* played, latent hypotheses, contribute as crucially to what evolves as what *is* done, offers paradigms for human affairs; and poems in this anthology show how richly thus suggestive chess can be. But any relationship between chess and life beyond it is entirely abstract and figurative. Whereas the supreme point of literature is that it explores, mediates and clarifies life itself, emerges from and takes as its ingredients man's 'natural and unalienable inheritance'; and in the great poets and novelists achieves our most profound and searching articulation of the human spirit.

Now, as C. H. O'D. Alexander observed,

Social chess is played for fun; competitive chess is work and very hard work indeed – and while it can give very deep satisfaction, it is the kind of satisfaction and fulfilment one gets from work, not play.[7]

Also, like poetry, chess for the serious practitioner is exceptionally taxing work not accredited as such by society generally. Compound with this stress the crucial difference that chess does not engage with life, and the serious player becomes a freak prone to extreme pressures indeed. G. K. Chesterton's remark, 'Poets do not go mad; but chess players do', if historically inaccurate in its first clause, embodies a true perception. The great poets seem on the whole a well-balanced orderly bunch compared to the great chess players. Five who would make anyone's list of the all-time top dozen players could fairly be described as, intermittently or terminally, mad. Paul Morphy, the original 'pride and sorrow of chess', after demonstrating in 1859 that at twenty-one he was overwhelmingly the world's best, resentful of his fame as 'a mere chess player' renounced the game and receded into reclusive decades of melancholic paranoia. Wilhelm Steinitz, World Champion from 1866–1894, ended his days convinced he could move chess pieces by impulses from his brain and defeat God at odds of pawn and move. Akiba Rubinstein, unlucky to be denied by Lasker a world title match he would probably have won, was paranoiac eventually to a point where he supposed other players and officials were intent on poisoning him, or would flee rooms others entered; incapacitated for formal play, he survived for decades shunning all social contacts. Alexander Alekhine, World Champion – except for two years – from 1927 until his death in 1946, the most single-minded and aggressive chess

[7] C. H. O'D. Alexander, *Fischer v Spassky, Reykjavik 1972*, 1972.

genius prior to Fischer, was outside his wonderfully creative play a monster of selfishness and crassness. After mysterious double-dealings he extricated himself from post-revolutionary Russia by a marriage of convenience, jettisoning his wife when he was safe. Two of his four subsequent wives were decades older than himself. Alekhine's chess manners included hurling pieces, smashing furniture, and once drunkenly urinating on the floor. He was an alcoholic. His last years were clouded by the appearance over his name in Nazi-occupied France of crazed ideological articles extolling 'Aryan' as opposed to morally depraved 'Jewish' chess (many of the world's greatest players have been Jews). Bobby Fischer, the most recent notable chess eccentric, recalls his American predecessor Morphy in that, precisely as he had established a dominance over his contemporaries unparalleled since Morphy, he tragically withdrew from play. Brought up by a mother with whom in adolescence he definitively quarrelled, thereafter a social isolate living in hotel rooms, Fischer is the most lopsided of all chess champions, appearing to remain humanly undeveloped outside a passion for the game which more totally absorbed his life than any other player's. He loved crushing opponents, remarking 'I like to see their egos crumble'; his rhetoric consisted of terms such as *smash*, *crunch*, *bam*. His egotistical fantasizing was extreme:

This little thing between me and Spassky, it's a microcosm of the whole world political situation. They always suggest that the two world leaders should fight it out hand to hand, and this is the kind of thing we are doing.

(Compare Lowell's poem 'The Winner', which non-chessplaying poetry-readers may not realize is an amalgam of Fischerisms.) Yet Fischer's lifelong extraordinary excesses of temperament and behaviour, his demands, protests and walk-outs, far from furthering his own chess cause first perversely delayed for perhaps a decade his becoming World Champion, then subsequently prevented him from capitalizing on his pre-eminence: despite his financial demands Fischer never collected the huge rewards possible after his defeat of Spassky. That triumph led only to the closure of his chess career at twenty-nine because the international chess world would not allow him arrogantly to dictate all terms.

How did characters so weird play such powerfully lucid chess? As Joseph Conrad notes in *The Shadow Line*, a mad carpenter will still make a sane box. In the 1920s the precocious Mexican chess-genius Torre flipped suddenly, removing all his clothes on a New York bus, and never recovered sanity. Visitors years later found his chess unimpaired. Ability at chess, or carpentry, in contrast to poetic achievement, is unaffected by the sanity of one's human attitudes, so long as one's state of mind or behaviour allows the activity at all.

Unsurprisingly, chess and its players have attracted psychoanalytical comment. In 1930 Freud's eminent follower Ernest Jones read to the British Psychoanalytical Society a paper, 'The Problem of Paul Morphy', in the course of which Jones found much material for comment in the game itself, seizing upon the crucial importance and vulnerability of the king to conclude that chess is 'adapted to gratify at the same time both the homosexual and antagonistic aspects of the father–son contest.'[8]

Reuben Fine, a candidate for Alekhine's title when the Second World War disrupted international chess, who subsequently forsook serious play for the profession of psychoanalysis, is uniquely placed to bring experience of play at the highest level to clinical discussion of chess. His book *The Psychology of the Chess Player* has small comfort for those of us who might prefer to believe the game's satisfactions innocent:

Chess is a contest between two men in which there is considerable ego involvement. In some ways it certainly touches upon the conflicts surrounding aggression, homosexuality, masturbation and narcissism.[9]

And, again, 'father–son rivalry'. The king's special status as a piece, its loss deciding the game regardless of other considerations, is a feature making chess unique among board games. The king therefore becomes 'the central figure in the symbolism of the game', deriving its meanings from its combination of all-importance and weakness: 'The King stands for: the boy's penis in the phallic stage, the self-image of the man, and the father cut down to boy's size.' Under the first head it 'rearouses the castration anxiety characteristic of that period'. The player prone to touch or fondle his own or captured pieces is subconsciously enacting masturbation or making a homosexual advance. Infantile omnipotence is another impulse offered huge scope by the nature of chess; and the role of the powerful queen attracts a further

[8] Ernest Jones, *Essays in Applied Psycho-analysis*, vol. I, 1951.
[9] Reuben Fine, *The Psychology of the Chess Player*, New York, 1967.

complex of psychoanalytical comment. Altogether chess is seen as enacting deeply repressed aggression, centred in and sublimating the Oedipal conflict: underlying the overt quest for checkmate is a basic ambition to expose as weak, castrate, and destroy the father. Fine notes that the intense aggressiveness inherent in the game is controlled and repressed by its procedures and etiquette: there is no physical aggression or even contact; the rules of serious play virtually exclude dialogue; and only at novice-level are games pursued until checkmate, itself a position short of actual capture of the king. As for any homosexual ingredients, 'overt homosexuality is almost unknown among chess players . . . This is all the more striking in that artists, with whom chess masters like to compare themselves, are so frequently homosexual.' Fine observes that where chess players' characteristically strong ego-control disintegrates before the underlying pressures, the symptoms tend to be 'paranoia, megalomania and exhibitionism'. A caricature-anticipation of Fischer's extravagant statement about playing Spassky occurs in a case Fine cites of psychotic breakdown in a chess player who in 1947, the year before the Soviet player Botvinnik in fact won the world title vacated by Alekhine's death, insisted: 'The real ruler of Russia is not Stalin but Botvinnik . . . I am going to go to Russia and beat Botvinnik. In this way I will conquer the world for America.'

Fine's later book on the Fischer–Spassky match[10] naturally finds the American genius, with whom Fine was early acquainted, whose sublimation in chess of all other gratifications was so total, rich material for clinical comment. Fischer's expressed desire 'to live the rest of my life in a house built exactly like a rook' moves Fine to offer 'a typical double symbolic meaning: first of all it is the strong penis for which he apparently finds so little use in real life; second, it is a castle in which he can live in grandiose fantasy, like the kings of old, shutting out the real world.'

Most of us woodpushers will not worry about the sinister proclivities psychoanalysts find lurking within our activity. Such interpretations of chess may, however, partly explain the decidedly inferior interest and ability in chess shown by women, who may be glad to be spared some of the necessary motivations. Certainly, as (in Fine's words) 'an intellectual aggression, a successful sublimation', chess is crucially a

[10] Reuben Fine, *Bobby Fischer's Conquest of the World's Chess Championship*, New York, 1973; London, 1975.

contest; and so affords special outlets for intellectual abilities whether or not a man also develops these in other areas. Compounding the game's innate aggressiveness is the tension generated by such factors as its behavioural restraints; the slowness of play yet inexorableness of the chess clock ticking away one's time; the fact that unlike a scientist who if one hypothesis fails in practice can try another, or the poet who can redraft endlessly, the chess player has to commit himself irrevocably to a single over-the-board move among the many he will have considered; the absoluteness of defeat or victory and the certainty that in a game devoid of chance one has only oneself to blame for the former. The etherealized aggression and constant nervous strain produce a players' rhetoric vehement beyond the simply military nature of some of the game's terminology. Fischer's style of verbal exultation is characteristic of many players at all levels. Defeat stings, and is rarely acknowledged with grace, explanations offered being usually in terms of one's own 'stupid' play or 'blunders' rather than the opponent's excellence. During play, the 'enemy' position is, with luck, 'ruined', until he is 'dead'; a passed pawn becomes 'enormous', a captured one is 'chopped', and so forth. I write this late on an evening in which I have won a ferocious game in my club championship, about which I admit to feeling exhilarating floods of satisfaction; but my polite inclination at the moment of victory to temper my real delight was reinforced by the taut silent fury on my opponent's face, as he swept immediately out looking as though he wanted to knife me. All he lacked was knives. Chess victory sweetens a day however troubled in other ways; while losing preys on one's sleep. The egotism of writers, which certainly exists, is less stark and more diffused; and mixed with a humbling sense of the complex intractability of life itself, which writing unlike chess engages and, if any good, has to acknowledge with exceptional openness.

Chess is certainly addictive, capable of becoming an obsession retarding or excluding achievement in other areas, as H. G. Wells understood:

The passion for playing chess is one of the most unaccountable in the world. It slaps the theory of natural selection in the face. . . . It annihilates a man. You have, let us say, a promising politician, a rising artist, that you wish to destroy. Dagger or bomb are archaic, clumsy and unreliable – but teach him, inoculate him with chess.[11]

[11] H. G. Wells, *Certain Personal Matters*, 1898.

Anyone who has seen the serious chess scene from inside will have encountered lives observably deformed by enslavement to the game. It is perhaps surprising that any among the really committed, their mental faculties weirdly subverted into the insulated, fascinating yet sterile depths and harmonies of struggle within the sixty-four-square world, has accomplished anything outside the game at all. As, last century, Henry James Byron succinctly put it, 'Life's too short for chess.'

I should perhaps here outline my own credentials for more than hearsay comment. Learning the moves at six, I really caught chess at about ten, and for three years was an addictive casual player against anyone chancing my way. I read chess books and played through games of the masters, and whiled away school lessons with a pocket-set concealed on the desk-seat between myself and my opponent. At eleven I wonderfully enjoyed beating a nineteen-year-old to top my school chess club ladder. It is characteristic of chess players' psychology that the sixth-formers running the club, loath to print in that term's school magazine a first-year pupil above them, listed me seventh. I abandoned the club and reverted to casual play. Of course chess at English schools now, partly because of the stimulus given by the 1972 Fischer–Spassky publicity, is vastly stronger and more organized than in the early 1950s. From age thirteen, when puberty ambushed me, until thirty-five, my chess-bug was dormant, though I knew it was there: I was a chess player the way an alcoholic who has stopped drinking is an alcoholic. Years elapsed between casual games; I followed only superficially even world title matches. My tertiary, though I hope not terminal, phase of reactivation, began when in 1976 a sort of chess epidemic broke out around the social areas of the New University of Ulster where I work. Since then my high-frequency casual chess has ranged from the carefully-fought, through lunch-hour chess-fixes, to lightning games late on at some party when to the astonishment of those remaining I and a like-minded soul start shoving wood about. And, at long last, I have succumbed to joining clubs. This discovers the more consuming, intensified and satisfying world of formal play with the chess clock adding an extra dimension. Fortunately, at forty, after my years of abstinence, I know that most of any chess future I might have had is safely behind me. Playing for a club team, or very occasionally in a weekend congress where one is obsessively at it morning, afternoon and evening, is exhilarating but controllable; I switch off, and turn to other things. I am a moderate club player, with at my level a certain talent for combative, complicating middle-game resourcefulness; and that is all.

Observing some of the chess-junkies I now meet, I am glad my own chess history precludes more serious temptation. But I know enough about that freakish phenomenon the serious chess mind to be impressed that, among the all-time greats, as well as the pure obsessives and madmen, any at all have developed other abilities. Philidor, the eighteenth century's greatest player, was also a composer of note. Staunton, the only Englishman so far with any claim to be, at his brief peak in the 1840s, the world's best, was a prominent Shakespearian scholar. Emanuel Lasker contributed to mathematics. Staunton and Lasker, however, withdrew from chess for sustained periods, and the Englishman was notoriously prickly, as when dishonourably avoiding a match against and certain defeat by Morphy during the latter's meteoric European visit, about any suggestion that he was other than a literary gentleman and chess amateur. Such a rôle is scarcely tenable since, over the past fifty years, the colossal proliferation of theory to be mastered for success at the highest levels. Reuben Fine had to abandon chess for another career. Top players nowadays are effectively full-time professionals, often supplementing their income from actual play by chess journalism, any other accomplishment a sideline.

There is, however, one twentieth-century example of a man who forsook exceptional achievement in another field for the obsessive pursuit of chess: the artist Marcel Duchamp, whose unique experience of success in both areas enabled him to make enlightening comments on similarities and differences between the creative processes and temperaments of art and chess. He is also, for discussion of the psychology of creativity in chess and in contrastingly life-orientated areas, an interestingly illuminating 'case'. It is significant, in the light of my general discussion so far, that Duchamp as an artist was at the furthest remove from any tradition of naturalism or conception of art as socially useful or in any normal sense for life's sake; from the Lawrencean conviction that 'the primary purpose of art is moral'. Born in 1887, Duchamp was an artistic ironist of the absurd, a Dadaist and surrealist associated with André Breton. He was notorious for painting moustaches on the Mona Lisa and exhibiting a urinal. His painting, after his earliest work, dehumanizes people in the interests of geometric or conceptual pattern and movement. His *Nude Descending a Staircase* is one of the archetypal 'modern' paintings. Painting itself

Duchamp came to find an unsatisfactory medium for his particular bent: 'It should have to do with the grey matter of our understanding instead of being purely visual.'[12] For his final major work, unfinished after several years, *The Bride Stripped Bare by Her Bachelors, Even* (generally known for convenience as *The Large Glass*), he abandoned traditional painter's materials altogether in striving to achieve, on glass, a wholly abstract rendering of his extremely complex conception. By this time he was turning increasingly to the wholly conceptual world of chess: in a letter of 1919 to the three Stettheimer sisters apologizing for failure to write earlier, Duchamp explains: 'My attention is so completely absorbed by chess. I play night and day and nothing in the world interests me more than finding the right move. . . . I like painting less and less.'

He had always known the game; some of his paintings, such as *Portrait of Chess Players*, took it for a theme. For an artist eager to eliminate the 'retinal' or 'visual' aspects of painting and translate it to a world of ideas and movement, committed to an ideology of art's social non-utility and to subversion through art of social and community values, and a corresponding personal life-style, the attraction of chess is evident. It was not, as for artists of a different philosophy, a contrastingly abstract realm of creativity, but virtually a consummation of his whole artistic enterprise, his desire for the profoundly useless. So too, for this particular artist,

The milieu of chess players is far more sympathetic than that of artists. These people are completely cloudy, completely blind, wearing blinkers . . . madmen of a certain quality, the way an artist is supposed to be, and isn't, in general.[13]

From his early thirties, Duchamp abandoned art for chess as a truly obsessive addict. Man Ray commented on Duchamp's marriage to Lydie Levassor-Sarrazin in 1927:

Duchamp spent most of the one week they lived together studying chess problems, and his bride, in desperate retaliation, got up one night when he was asleep and glued the chess pieces to the board. They were divorced three months later.[14]

[12] Duchamp quotations, except where otherwise indicated, are from Arturo Schwarz, *The Complete Works of Marcel Duchamp*, 1969.
[13] Pierre Cabanne, *Dialogues with Marcel Duchamp*, tr. Ron Padgett, 1971.
[14] Man Ray, quoted in Pierre Cabanne, *op. cit.*

Another friend, Roché, remarked: 'He needed a good chess game just as a baby needs his bottle.'

One notices that Duchamp's access of interest coincided with the advent of chess equivalents to Dadaism and surrealism, the 'hyper-modernism' of Réti and others, who revolutionized chess theory and practice by showing that all the accepted orthodox principles – advancing centre pawns, not moving a piece twice in the opening, or the queen early – could be successfully flouted in the interests of more devious strategies. Predictably, he greatly admired Nimzowitsch. Duchamp's serious chess career began with his return to France from the USA in 1923. He finished high in the French Championship several times; played for France in Chess Olympiads, alongside the naturalized Frenchman Alekhine; and won, for example, the Paris tournament of 1932 ahead of Znosko-Borovsky. He was essentially a profound positional player, with a predilection for the endgame where with the board uncluttered the logical element in chess creativity predominates. His one chess book, *Opposition and Sister Squares are Reconciled*,[15] studies king and pawn endings, the most pared-down of all. It is also characteristic of Duchamp in its artistic perversity: he commented, 'Chess champions never read this book, because the problem it poses never really turns up more than once in a lifetime. These are possible endgame problems, but they're so rare that they're almost Utopian.'

As an artist so intent upon purities of introverted abstraction that he more or less resented the necessity for the painter's creativity to end in something so crassly external as an actual picture, Duchamp was pleased that 'in chess there are some extremely beautiful things in the domain of movement, but not in the visual domain. It is the imagining of the movement or of the gesture that makes the beauty, in this case. It's completely in one's grey matter.'[16]

In these terms, he finds that chess creativity has greater affinities with musical composition, and poetry, where the external visual element – ink marks on paper – is the sketchiest notation of created beauty:

Objectively, a game of chess looks very much like a pen-and-ink drawing, with the difference, however, that the chess player paints with black and white forms already prepared instead of inventing forms as does the artist. The design thus

[15] Marcel Duchamp and Vitaly Halberstadt, *Opposition and Sister Squares are Reconciled*, Brussels, 1932.

[16] Pierre Cabanne, *op. cit*.

formed on the chessboard has apparently no visual aesthetic value, and is more like a score for music which can be played again and again. Beauty in chess does not seem to be a visual experience as in painting. Beauty in chess is closer to beauty in poetry; the chess pieces are the block alphabet which shapes thoughts, and these thoughts, although making a visual design on the chessboard, express their beauty *abstractly*, like a poem. Actually, I believe that every chess player experiences a mixture of two aesthetic pleasures: first, the abstract image akin to the poetic idea of writing; secondly, the sensuous pleasure of the ideographic execution of that image on the chessboard. From my close contact with artists and chess players I have come to the conclusion that while all artists are not chess players, all chess players are artists.

Of course, the analogy of creative conception and execution in chess and in poetry is confined to the aesthetic level, and ignores the crucial distinguishing features of chess as a contest for victory, poetry as engagement with life beyond the poem. In his conversations with Pierre Cabanne, Duchamp typically not so much acknowledges, as rejoices in, the fact that in chess 'there is no social purpose. That above all is important.'

Duchamp, exemplifying creativity in the two areas, emerges as an illustration of much that I have suggested both about the disparate psychological motivations of chess and the humane arts, and of their connection within the purely aesthetic realm of creative delight. Artists of a different stamp from Duchamp, working within the central tradition of painting as exploration and illumination of experience, would by no means have found addiction to chess so consonant with their artistic principles and quests. Yet, in concluding this discussion, it must be insisted too that, more than any other sport or game chess resembles writing, painting and music in being an obsessional mental activity preoccupied with exploring tension and complication to resolve them to triumphant harmony, eliciting unified pattern from diversity; so that in the greatest chess creations, as in art or poetry, beauty and truth are felt to become cathartically one.

My arrangement of this anthology in six sections brings together poems offering variations on similar themes or subject-areas, using chess metaphor to treat of, for example, personal relationships, or social and historical matters. But of course poems resist limiting categories; those in any one section may partake of the preoccupations of another; and my groupings should be understood only as reflecting emphases. Even within my sections on 'The Game' and 'Players', chess being what it suggestively is life and attitudes to it insinuate themselves. And John Fuller's striking long poem 'The Most Difficult Position', although about the chess players Staunton and Morphy, dramatizes so many larger human motivations in exploring its protagonists as complex individuals whose relationship happened to occur within the precisely definable area of chess rivalry, that the poem most appropriately belongs in the section entitled 'Personal Relationships'.

Looking historically at the ways chess metaphor has been used to talk about life, one finds predictably that the medieval period seized on its potential for figurative sermonizings about man's mortal condition in the cosmic game:

> Farewell, this world is but a Cherry Fair . . .
> Tyll sotell deth knokyd at my gate,
> And on-avysed he seyd to me, chek-mate!

we are told in one piece collected in Carleton Browne's *Religious Lyrics of the Fifteenth Century*; and in another,

> Yit in a whyle, thu schall be cheke-mate;
> When deth wyll come and take hys propour fe,
> Than schall thu know thi pride was vanyte!

Although my excerpt from Chaucer's *Book of the Duchess* wittily allegorizes life as a chess game lost inexorably to 'Fortune', commonly in medieval writing the context is specifically Christian. And while chess supplied useful imagery for fulminations about the pettiness and transience of man within God's designs, the game itself incurred the church's disapproval, as profane self-indulgence; partly because it occasioned much gambling, but primarily because churchmen were shrewdly aware of its extraordinary power to obsess adherents and distract them from, for example, religious duties. Not that ecclesiastics were immune: the following lament by a seventeenth-century churchman, quoted from *The Harleyan Miscellany* in Reuben Fine's *The Psychology of the Chess Player*, will occasion wry recognition in modern addicts:

It is a great time-waster. How many precious hours (which can never be recalled) have I profusely spent in this game. It hath had with me a fascinating property. I have been bewitched by it: when I have begun, I have not had the power to give over. It hath not done with me, when I have done with it. It hath followed me into my study, into my pulpit; when I have been praying or preaching, I have (in my thoughts) been playing at chess. . . . It hath caused me to break many solemn promises. . . . It hath wounded my conscience and broken my peace. . . .

While from Cowley's ode 'Destiny' through to R. S. Thomas's 'Play' chess continues to provide a framework for specifically religious poetry, by the Renaissance secularization of the human-condition theme becomes normal:

> For deadly hate
> Did play checkmate
> With me, poor pawn

wrote George Gascoigne, the Elizabethan whose poetry so engagingly admits himself to be the complete 'Renaissance man' failed on all fronts of courtly endeavour except writing it up.

In Surrey's fine 'To the Lady that Scorned Her Lover', chess as metaphor for a love-relationship enters English poetry; perhaps surprisingly late, for the theme had occurred in Arabic literature, and in medieval Europe chess was a feminine as well as masculine aristocratic pastime. Froissart's fourteenth-century *Chronicle* has a long prose account of a game between Edward III and the Countess of Salisbury for whom he had a passion; and the game seems traditionally to have featured in romantic courtship. Surrey's use of chess in love-poetry for long had few successors. There is Spenser's single generalizing line in *The Shepherd's Calendar*, 'Love they him called, that gave me checkmate'; a brief Shakespearian reference of which more later; Middleton's extraordinary dramatized set piece in *Women Beware Women*; then, in the nineteenth century, Keats's vignette in 'The Cap and Bells':

> She cried for chess – I played a game with her,
> Castled her king with such a vixen look,
> It bodes ill to his Majesty.

But from Bulwer Lytton's 'The Chess Board', and particularly in recent decades of the twentieth century, chess as figurative of that other trap-infested, sometimes combative, two-handed game of love, has evolved something of a tradition.

Chess comes also to provide poetic metaphor for events in the public world and life of society, including of course, in such a poem as Joseph Campbell's 'Chesspieces' set in the Irish troubles, war.

Particularly among the poems I have grouped as 'Moralities', the power of a pawn on reaching the eighth rank to 'promote' is a recurring theme for comment. Over the centuries one notices, as token of advance from an aristocratic towards a democratic society, a shift from the assumption in William Jones's *Caissa* that other pieces 'die with rapture if they save their king', to W. Cook Spens's vigorous pastiche-Burns 'A Pawn's a Pawn for A' That' or Peter Jay's 'Life of a Pawn', where the thrust of the message is the potential of pawns for rising to, or overthrowing, eminence, and their humble but indispensable collective industry.

As for the game itself, the colourful account of play between Hermes and Apollo in Goldsmith's version of Vida's *Scacchia Ludus*, evidently a blunder-riddled romantically primitive performance, dramatizes a succession of taunts, gamesmanship, attempted cheating, protests and final victorious gloating that attests Vida's acuteness about chess psychology. Things have changed little in the centuries between these nefarious goings-on, and recent contests such as Spassky–Fischer 1972, Korchnoi–Spassky 1977, and Karpov–Korchnoi 1978, conducted amid mutual recrimination, antics like Spassky's insistence on playing invisibly from inside his 'booth' and wearing a tennis visor, and accusations of everything from hypnotism to coded yoghourt. Chess competitors do anything almost-illegal to avoid the agony of defeat; although nowadays, while Korchnoi has alleged that former World Champion Petrosian kicks him under the table, it is perhaps rare for players to smite opponents dead with the chessboard, as occurs in *The Romance of Guy of Warwick*. Doubtless the Soviet chess authorities would welcome any mishap which spared their players the embarrassment of having to defend the world title against the Russian defector Korchnoi, so much more famous in his chess-possessed nation than Solzhenitsyn.

Researching poetry for 'chessy' material has been enjoyable, often leading me to roam the works of poets I might otherwise have neglected to read or re-read. The major English poets, despite Chaucer's early example, disappoint until recent times by mentioning the game only fleetingly; though Tennyson makes extended metaphoric use of chess in verse plays, and in a single line in 'The Princess', 'And had our wine and chess beneath the planes', notes a mixture of activities less uncommon than non-players might suppose. Byron, who in *Don Juan* remarks 'Good company's a chess board', unfortunately offers no further comment on a game one suspects he might have relished. From Milton one expected nothing: seventeenth-century puritanism scorned the game as frivolity, and very likely thought the wooden pieces themselves smacked of popery. Shakespeare's one direct reference is in *The Tempest*:

> *Here Prospero discovers Ferdinand and Miranda playing at chess.*
> MIR.   Sweet lord, you play me false.
> FERD.   No, my dearest love,
>   I would not for the world.
> MIR.   Yes, for a score of kingdoms you should wrangle,
>   And I would call it fair.

This, at the moment of reconciliation between the pair, presenting chess as a paradigm of the deviously ambivalent love-relationship, implies a shrewd understanding of the game, as well as of human psychology.

But among the established poets of past centuries, it is the interesting minor talents, such as Surrey, Lovelace and Cowley, who write of chess or use its imagery at substantial length. With the twentieth century, the picture changes and more of the important figures offer usable material. Eliot, who does not, nevertheless of course provided an overall metaphor for section II of *The Waste Land* simply by entitling it 'A Game of Chess', referring in his notes to Middleton's chess *tour de force* in *Women Beware Women*.

A large proportion of the poetry in this anthology, however, dates from after 1950; a fact reflecting the wide diffusion of the game in recent decades. In the middle ages it belonged to the courtly, prowess at chess being routinely attributed, doubtless without justification, to kings and nobles, so that to this day in Russia the chess king is called 'Korol' after Charlemagne, whose reputation for playing the game is almost certainly merely a flattering literary fiction. In the eighteenth and nineteenth centuries chess was a property of the educated clientele of coffee houses and universities, then few. Today, even in England, it can be found almost anywhere. Tracking the 'chess poetry' of the past few decades was necessarily an enterprise in which I had to rely on memory and reading around, unaided by concordances and other reference works; and I would thank here the very many people who responded to appeals for information printed in some magazines. I should also particularly thank Patricia Beer for kindly permitting me to reprint the poem 'Checkmate' from her first collection *Loss of the Magyar*, despite it being, she now feels, work in a manner she has long outgrown. Finally, I am gratefully indebted to Peter Jay of the Anvil Press, not only for publishing this anthology, but for having the idea in the first place.

ANDREW WATERMAN
1981

Note on the Texts

SPELLING has been modernized in poems from the Elizabethan period or later, in the interests of reader-convenience and to avoid the air of false quaintness given by obsolete spellings of words which with very few exceptions remain current in the language. In earlier poetry, where spelling is inseparable from the nature and texture of the language as it then was, modernization would be deformation; obsolete words and forms have been glossed.

Punctuation, the principles of which show continual slight modification through the centuries, but which occasions no confusion, has been left as it appears in the printed source for a poem (see Bibliography), which means that in the case of medieval poems and extracts and a few of somewhat later date, it is in fact supplied or amended by a modern editor.

Titles printed in italic type have been supplied by the present editor for excerpts from longer poems and plays.

Within each section the poets are represented in chronological order.

A.W.

1   *The Game*

The Playe Most Gloryous

And there was founde by clerkes full prudent
Of the chess the playe most gloryous,
Whiche is so sotill and so mervaylous
That it were harde the matter to discryve,
For though a man studied all his lyve
He shall aye fynde dyverse fantasyes,
There is therein so great diversytie. . . .

JOHN LYDGATE

from *Troy Book*, II, 806–812

Outwitted

To alle folkys vertuouse,
That gentil ben and amerouse,
Which love the faire pley notable
Of the chesse, most delytable,
Whith alle her hoole ful entente:
To hem thys boke y will presente;
Where they shal fynde and sen Anoon,
How that I, nat yore agoon,
Was of a Fers so Fortunat
Into a corner dryve and maat,
Of hire that, withoute lye,
Koude ful many iupartye,
And hir draughtes in swich wise
So disposen and devise
That ulixes, to reknen alle,
To hir was nat peregalle.

J OHN LYDGATE

from *Reson and Sensuallyte*, lines 1–16

her] *their*   Fers] *chess piece*: '*counsellor' or queen*   hire] *her*   iupartye] *problem*
in chess   draughtes] *moves*   ulixes] *Ulysses*   peregalle] *fully equal*

The Chess Play

A secret many years unseen,
In play at Chess, who knows the game,
First of the King, and then the Queen,
Knight, Bishop, Rook, and so by name,
    Of every Pawn I will descry,
    The nature with the quality.

The King

The King himself is haughty care,
Which overlooketh all his men,
And when he seeth how they fare,
He steps among them now and then,
    Whom, when his foe presumes to check,
    His servants stand, to give the neck.

The Queen

The Queen is quaint, and quick conceit,
Which makes her walk which way she list,
And roots them up, that lie in wait
To work her treason, ere she wist:
    Her force is such against her foes,
    That whom she meets, she overthrows.

The Knight

The Knight is knowledge how to fight
Against his prince's enemies,
He never makes his walk outright,
But leaps and skips, in wily wise,
    To take by sleight a traitorous foe,
    Might slily seek their overthrow.

neck] *move to cover check*   quaint] *ingenious*   conceit] *conception*

The Bishop

The Bishop he is witty brain,
That chooseth crossest paths to pace,
And evermore he pries with pain,
To see who seeks him most disgrace:
    Such stragglers when he finds astray,
    He takes them up, and throws away.

The Rooks

The Rooks are reason on both sides,
Which keep the corner houses still,
And warily stand to watch their tides,
By secret art to work their will,
    To take sometime a thief unseen,
    Might mischief mean to King or Queen.

The Pawns

The Pawn before the King, is peace,
Which he desires to keep at home,
Practice, the Queen's, which does not cease
Amid the world abroad to roam,
    To find, and fall upon each foe,
    Whereas his mistress means to go.

Before the Knight, is peril placed,
Which he, by skipping overgoes,
And yet that Pawn can work a cast,
To overthrow his greatest foes;
    The Bishop's prudence, prying still,
    Which way to work his master's will.

The Rooks' poor Pawns, are silly swains,
Which seldom serve, except by hap,
And yet those Pawns, can lay their trains,
To catch a great man, in a trap:
   So that I see, sometimes a groom
   May not be spared from his room.

The Nature of the Chess Men

The King is stately, looking high;
The Queen, doth bear like majesty:
The Knight, is hardy, valiant, wise,
The Bishop, prudent, and precise:
   The Rooks, no rangers out of ray,
   The Pawns, the pages in the play.

L'ENVOY

Then rule with care, and quick conceit,
And fight with knowledge, as with force;
So bear a brain, to dash deceit,
And work with reason and remorse:
   Forgive a fault, when young men play,
   So give a mate, and go your way.

And when you play beware of check,
Know how to save and give a neck:
And with a check, beware of mate;
But chief, ware had I wist too late:
   Lose not the Queen, for ten to one,
   If she be lost, the game is gone.

NICHOLAS BRETON

ray] *array*

from Chess Play

And Mercury long afterward
   in travel, as I guess,
Did teach the men of Italy
   to play this game of chess.
For, landed on the Italian shore,
   as ancient stories tell,
He spied by chance a lonely dame,
   that liked him passing well,
And seeing her and liking her,
   he loved her withal;
This was a brave Sereian nymph,
   whom Scacchis men did call:
Who while she kept her snowy swans
   about the rivers wild,
He spied, and loved and lay with her,
   and got the maid with child.
And to requite such courtesy,
   showed by so kind a dame:
To drive away the time withal,
   he taught her first this game,
And for the loss of liberty,
   and maidenhead withal:
Of her name Scacchis Scacchia
   this play at chess did call.
And that this god in memory
   the lass might longer have
A boxen chess-board gilded round
   unto the girl he gave,
And taught her cunning in the same,
   to play the game by art.
Which after to the country swains
   this lady did impart:

Mercury] i.e. Hermes: cf. Goldsmith's translation

Who taught their late posterity
 to use this kind of play,
A game of great antiquity
 still used at this day.

 G. B. (1597)

translated from *Scacchia Ludus*
by MARCO GIROLAMO VIDA (1485–1566)

To Dr F. B. On his Book of Chess

Sir, now unravelled is the Golden Fleece:
Men that could only fool at fox and geese
Are new made politicians by thy book,
And both can judge and conquer with a look.
The hidden fate of princes you unfold;
Court, clergy, commons, by your law controlled;
 Strange, serious wantoning, all that they
   Blustered, and cluttered for, *you play*.

RICHARD LOVELACE

from Vida's Game of Chess

[*Phoebus Apollo wants a move back; Hermes cheats* — ED.]

Fired at this great success, with double rage
Apollo hurries on his troops to engage,
For blood and havoc wild; and, while he leads
His troops thus careless, loses both his steeds:
For if some adverse warriors were o'erthrown,
He little thought what dangers threat his own.
But slyer Hermes with observant eyes
Marched slowly cautious, and at distance spies
What moves must next succeed, what dangers next arise.
Often would he, the stately Queen to snare,
The slender Foot to front her arms prepare,
And to conceal his scheme he sighs and feigns
Such a wrong step would frustrate all his pains.
Just then an Archer, from the right-hand view,
At the pale Queen his arrow boldly drew,
Unseen by Phoebus, who, with studious thought,
From the left side a vulgar hero brought.
But tender Venus, with a pitying eye,
Viewing the sad destruction that was nigh,
Winked upon Phoebus (for the Goddess sat
By chance directly opposite); at that
Roused in an instant, young Apollo threw
His eyes around the field his troops to view;
Perceived the danger, and with sudden fright
Withdrew the Foot that he had sent to fight,
And saved his trembling Queen by seasonable flight.
But Maia's son with shouts filled all the coast:
The Queen, he cried, the important Queen is lost.
Phoebus, howe'er, resolving to maintain
What he had done, bespoke the heavenly train.
   What mighty harm, in sportive mimic fight,
Is it to set a little blunder right,
When no preliminary rule debarred?

Foot] *pawn(s)*   Archer] *bishop*

44

If you henceforward, Mercury, would guard
Against such practice, let us make the law:
And whosoe'er shall first to battle draw,
Or white, or black, remorseless let him go
At all events, and dare the angry foe.
   He said, and this opinion pleased around:
Jove turned aside, and on his daughter frowned,
Unmarked by Hermes, who, with strange surprise,
Fretted and foamed, and rolled his ferret eyes,
And but with great reluctance could refrain
From dashing at a blow all off the plain.
Then he resolved to interweave deceits, –
To carry on the war by tricks and cheats.
Instant he called an Archer from the throng,
And bid him like the courser wheel along:
Bounding he springs, and threats the pallid Queen.
The fraud, however, was by Phoebus seen;
He smiled, and, turning to the Gods, he said:
Though, Hermes, you are perfect in your trade,
And you can trick and cheat to great surprise,
These little sleights no more shall blind my eyes;
Correct them if you please, the more you thus disguise.
The circle laughed aloud; and Maia's son
(As if it had but by mistake been done)
Recalled his Archer, and with motion due
Bid him advance, the combat to renew.
But Phoebus watched him with a jealous eye,
Fearing some trick was ever lurking nigh,
For he would oft, with sudden sly design,
Send forth at once two combatants to join
His warring troops, against the law of arms,
Unless the wary foe was ever in alarms.

267–331

[Bishop takes knight; pawn takes bishop]

Glittering in arms from far a courser came,
Threatened at once the King and Royal Dame;
Thought himself safe when he the post had seized,
And with the future spoils his fancy pleased.
Fired at the danger a young Archer came,
Rushed on his foe, and levelled sure his aim;
(And though a Pawn his sword in vengeance draws,
Gladly he'd lose his life in glory's cause).
The whistling arrow to his bowels flew,
And the sharp steel his blood profusely drew;
He drops the reins, he totters to the ground,
And his life issued murmuring through the wound.
Pierced by the Foot, this Archer bit the plain;
The Foot himself was by another slain;
And with inflamed revenge, the battle burns again.

338–352

[Holocaust]

But in the midst of all the battle raged
The snowy Queen, with troops at once engaged;
She felled an Archer as she sought the plain, –
As she retired an Elephant was slain:
To right and left her fatal spears she sent,
Burst through the ranks, and triumphed as she went;
Through arms and blood she seeks a glorious fate,
Pierces the farthest lines, and nobly great
Leads on her army with a gallant show,
Breaks the battalions, and cuts through the foe.
At length the sable King his fears betrayed,
And begged his military consort's aid:
With cheerful speed she flew to his relief,
And met in equal arms the female chief.
Who first, great Queen, and who at last did bleed?
How many whites lay gasping on the mead?

Elephant] *rook*

46

Half dead, and floating in a bloody tide,
Foot, Knights, and Archer lie on every side.
Who can recount the slaughter of the day?
How many leaders threw their lives away?
The chequered plain is filled with dying box,
Havoc ensues, and with tumultuous shocks
The different coloured ranks in blood engage,
And Foot and Horse promiscuously rage.

368–391

[*More cheating*]

But Thracian Mars, in steadfast friendship joined
To Hermes, as near Phoebus he reclined,
Observed each chance, how all their motions bend,
Resolved if possible to serve his friend.
He a Foot-soldier and a Knight purloined
Out from the prison that the dead confined;
And slyly pushed 'em forward on the plain;
The enlivened combatants their arms regain,
Mix in the bloody scene, and boldly war again.
   So the foul hag, in screaming wild alarms
O'er a dead carcase muttering her charms,
(And with her frequent and tremendous yell
Forcing great Hecate from out of hell)
Shoots in the corpse a new fictitious soul;
With instant glare the supple eyeballs roll,
Again it moves and speaks, and life informs the whole.
   Vulcan alone discerned the subtle cheat;
And wisely scorning such a base deceit,
Called out to Phoebus. Grief and rage assail
Phoebus by turns; detected Mars turns pale.
Then awful Jove with sullen eye reproved
Mars, and the captives ordered to be moved
To their dark caves; bid each fictitious spear
Be straight recalled, and all be as they were.

400–423

box] *boxwood*

47

[*Royal re-marriage*]

The afflicted Kings bewail their consorts dead,
And loathe the thoughts of a deserted bed;
And though each monarch studies to improve
The tender memory of his former love,
Their state requires a second nuptial tie.
Hence the pale ruler with a love-sick eye
Surveys the attendants of his former wife,
And offers one of them a royal life.
These, when their martial mistress had been slain,
Weak and despairing tried their arms in vain;
Willing, howe'er, amidst the Black to go,
They thirst for speedy vengeance on the foe.
Then he resolves to see who merits best,
By strength and courage, the imperial vest;
Points out the foe, bids each with bold design
Pierce through the ranks, and reach the deepest line:
For none must hope with monarchs to repose
But who can first, through thick surrounding foes,
Through arms and wiles, with hazardous essay,
Safe to the farthest quarters force their way.
Fired at the thought, with sudden, joyful pace
They hurry on; but first of all the race
Runs the third right-hand warrior for the prize, –
The glittering crown already charms her eyes.
Her dear associates cheerfully give o'er
The nuptial chase; and swift she flies before,
And Glory lent her wings, and the reward in store.
Nor would the sable King her hopes prevent,
For he himself was on a Queen intent,
Alternate, therefore, through the field they go.
Hermes led on, but by a step too slow,
His fourth left Pawn: and now the adventurous White
Had marched through all, and gained the wished for site.
Then the pleased King gives orders to prepare
The crown, the sceptre, and the royal chair,
And owns her for his Queen: around exult
The snowy troops, and o'er the Black insult.

Hermes burst into tears, – with fretful roar
Filled the wide air, and his gay vesture tore.

465–503

[*Pressurized by gamesmanship, Apollo misses a win*]

But the bold Queen, victorious, from behind
Pierces the foe; yet chiefly she designed
Against the King himself some fatal aim,
And full of war to his pavilion came.
Now here she rushed, now there; and had she been
But duly prudent, she had slipped between,
With course oblique, into the fourth white square,
And the long toil of war had ended there,
The King had fallen, and all his sable state;
And vanquished Hermes cursed his partial fate.
For thence with ease the championess might go,
Murder the king, and none could ward the blow.
With silence, Hermes, and with panting heart,
Perceived the danger, but with subtle art,
(Lest he should see the place) spurs on the foe,
Confounds his thoughts, and blames his being slow.
For shame! move on; would you for ever stay?
What sloth is this, what strange perverse delay? –
How could you e'er my little pausing blame? –
What! you would wait till night shall end the game?
Phoebus, thus nettled, with imprudence slew
A vulgar Pawn, but lost his nobler view.

525–546

[*Victory*]

Sole stood the King, the midst of all the plain,
Weak and defenceless, his companions slain. . . .
The Black King watched him with observant eye,
Followed him close, but left him room to fly.
Then when he saw him take the farthest line,
He sent the Queen his motions to confine,

49

And guard the second rank, that he could go
No farther now than to that distant row.
The sable monarch then with cheerful mien
Approached, but always with one space between.
But as the King stood o'er against him there,
Helpless, forlorn, and sunk in his despair,
The martial Queen her lucky moment knew,
Seized on the farthest seat with fatal view,
Nor left the unhappy King a place to flee unto.
At length in vengeance her keen sword she draws,
Slew him, and ended thus the bloody cause:
And all the gods around approved it with applause.
 The victor could not from his insults keep,
But laughed and sneered to see Apollo weep.

622–623; 640–657

OLIVER GOLDSMITH

translated from *Scacchia Ludus*
by MARCO GIROLAMO VIDA (1485–1566)

from Caissa

Square eight times eight in equal order lie,
These bright as snow, those dark with sable dye,
Like the broad target by the tortoise born,
Or like the hide by spotted panthers worn.
Then from a chest, with harmless heroes stored,
O'er the smooth plain two well-wrought hosts he poured;
The champions burned their rivals to assail,
Twice eight in black, twice eight in milkwhite mail;
In shape and station different, as in name,
Their motions various, nor their power the same.
Say, muse! (for Jove has nought from thee concealed)
Who formed the legions on the level field?

   High in the midst the reverend kings appear,
And o'er the rest their pearly scepters rear:
With solemn steps, majestically slow,
They gravely move, and shun the dangerous foe;
If e'er they call, the watchful subjects spring,
And die with rapture if they save their king,
On him the glory of the day depends,
He once imprisoned, all the conflict ends.

   The queens exulting near their consorts stand,
Each bears a deadly falchion in her hand;
Now here, now there, they bound with furious pride,
And thin the trembling ranks from side to side,
Swift as Camilla flying o'er the main,
Or lightly skimming o'er the dewy plain:
Fierce as they seem, some bold Plebeian spear
May pierce their shield, or stop their full career.

   55–82

'A god requests.' – He spake, and Sport obeyed.
He framed a tablet of celestial mold,

Inlayed with squares of silver and of gold;
Then of two metals formed the warlike band,
That here compact in show of battle stand;
He taught the rules that guide the pensive game,
And called it *Cassa* from the Dryad's name:
(Whence Albion's sons, who most its praise confess,
Approved the play, and named it thoughtful Chess.)

180—188

Now flies the monarch of the sable shield,
His legions vanquished, o'er the lonely field:
So when the morn, by rosy coursers drawn,
With pearls and rubies sows the verdant lawn,
Whilst each pale star from heaven's blue vault retires,
Still Venus gleams, and last of all expires.
He hears, where'er he moves, the dreadful sound;
Check the deep vales, and *Check* the woods rebound.
No place remains: he sees the certain fate,
And yields his throne to ruin, and Checkmate.

315—324

SIR WILLIAM JONES

The Game of the Pawn and the Queen

They may sing of the bat and the wicket,
   Or the racquet and net on the green,
But what are lawn tennis and cricket,
   To the game of the Pawn and the Queen!
The gun is a tyrant and slayer,
   The niblick a joy for the few;
Give me chess with a chivalrous player,
   And a fig for what others may do!

In summer when perfume of roses
   Blows in at the half-open door;
When the volume unwillingly closes,
   And talking is voted a bore;
Then oh for some leafy pavilion,
   Some bower the hot rays never drench,
With a friend deeply versed in Sicilian,
   And the intricate web of the French!

And in winter, when dismal and dreary
   The snow flakes fall thick in the street;
When newsboys limp haggard and weary,
   And policemen take nips on their beat;
Then whether it thaws or it freezes,
   For a nook by a warm-giving flame,
With the boxwood and ebony pieces
   And a comrade adept at the game!

ANONYMOUS (early 20th century)

The Sea and Chess

Silence. And silence still.
Then one long roller breaks,
And Hastings' houses fill
With the wild sound it makes.

Silence again. The sea,
Though it may seem to sleep,
Is still the vast and free
Inscrutable old deep.

Who shall entirely scan
All its mysteriousness?
Even the mind of man
Has deeps beyond our guess.

So, when a move has brought
Some strategy in sight,
We cannot plumb the thought
That brought that move to light.

And, small although it be,
And missed by careless eyes,
A chessboard, like the sea,
Has unplumbed mysteries.

Lord Dunsany

The Game of Chess

DOGMATIC STATEMENT CONCERNING THE GAME OF CHESS:
THEME FOR A SERIES OF PICTURES

Red knights, brown bishops, bright queens,
Striking the board, falling in strong 'L's' of colour.
Reaching and striking in angles,
        holding lines in one colour.
This board is alive with light;
        these pieces are living in form,
Their moves break and reform the pattern:
        luminous green from the rooks,
Clashing with 'X's' of queens,
        looped with the knight-leaps.

'Y' pawns, cleaving, embanking!
Whirl! Centripetal! Mate! King down in the vortex,
Clash, leaping of bands, straight strips of hard colour,
Blocked lights working in. Escapes. Renewal of contest.

EZRA POUND

Checkmate

It is daylight.
– And my brave men?
– Their ranks were gashed:
The horsemen came,
They cleaved our ranks;
Not one fell back!
– Those black prelates!
We are the played.
– The castle's razed,
The Queen is safe;
There is no death. . . .
It is daylight.
– Always this threat –
Those black prelates!
The King is dead?
– There is no death. . . .
– Always this threat!

R. H. MORRISON

Games

Like real kings once, with faces. The peaceful game
Was a clear substitute for battle. Now
This hopping horse has shed the knight, his name,
Mace-swinging swordsmen are reduced to slow

Formalized movements in the ruled calm
Of wooden symbols. The foot-slogging peon
Is still sacrificed without a royal qualm,
But only for strict advantage, for no common

Ranker or king really is an island here,
And one false moving pawn can undermine
The whole state's health. The game's so clear
Of pointless accident, for accidents illumine

The missed logic. Here lies the fascination,
When the play of possibilities ensures
No game repeats: the absorbed abstraction
In a locked field where no battle cures

Sick violence in a blood-letting crisis.
In intense theatres including more or less
Of chance and violence, on ranked terraces
Faces wooden with repetition and emptiness

Of real lives are gripped to passion, charged
With purpose, and the lost, dispersed feeling
Is revived, contracted to a stage, enlarged,
And death gives the ritual drama its whole meaning.

JACK CAREY

Carved Pieces

Carved pieces bend and step across the board
In stately cautiousness. I love this world
Of formal thought and fireside and pearled
Rook-battlements and how one can't afford
Queen-sacrifices if one's less insured
In skill and guile than he. My knight is curled
Now round behind the centre squares, pawns furled
And woven through his line while his adored
King fianchetto gently breaks that side
Like dry ice slowly melting into floes.
His bishops soon hold both diagonals,
His rook the seventh, my defence is wide,
And my game lost in only twenty goes.
My king adds one more to its funerals.

J. P. WARD

Medieval Chess King

Someone turned the key
Of the chambered stone
Where the chess king lay.

He was carved hartshorn.
In the hole of his eyes
Burned a garnet stone.

Disfigured he was
With the emerald vein
Of lichen on bone.

Who can say
What burial tinct
Wore his crown away

When dragon and drawn sword
The elements defy
So slenderly?

I laid him in my hand.
What was it went
O narrowly to the bone?

Remembered chequerings,
The games through Time
Of all chess kings.

PAULINE STAINER

Chess

So often men compare this game to war,
  Opposing camps in their array of wood,
That one forgets it is a game, no more,
  Without the loss, the tragedy, the blood.
If I allow it is a game inspired
  By eye for ground and wits to seize a chance,
    If I allow that singleness of mind
      And nerve is much required,
    Still it's not war but music's abstract dance
      Offers the truest analogue, I find.

Both have their transpositions and their traps,
  And chords or combinations which decide
New possibilities, surprises, gaps,
  For which imagination must provide.
Bach's counterpoint or Tal's attacking flair,
  Beethoven's bagatelles or Spassky's schemes,
    Insistent forks and pins or fifths and thirds,
      These different patterns share
    The deathless vigour of ideas and themes
      Developed and resolved – but not with words.

J. A. WAREING

2   *Players*

King Richard

The messengers them hyed harde
Tyll they came to Kynge Rycharde.
They founde Kynge Rycharde playe
At the chesse in his galaye;
The Erle of Rychemonde with hym played,
And Rycharde wan all that he layed.

ANONYMOUS (14th century)

from *Richard Cuer de Lyon*, lines 2181–2186

Close of Play

The sowdon sone rose up full ryght
(Syr Sowdan of Perce he hyght):
'Faber,' quod Sowdan, 'y bydde the
To playe at the chesses wyth me.'
'Syr,' quod he, 'wyth myn entente
I schall do yowre comawndement.'
To Faber chaumber there they wente
And aftur the chesses soon they sente.
They sate downe frendys in all wyse,
But they were wrothe, or they dud ryse.
Syr Faber at the chesses a worde seyde:
Sowdan was wrothe and owte brayde

Sowdan] *Sultan*   hyght] *was named*   entente] *wish, desire*   or] *before*
brayde] *moved quickly, started*

And clepyd hym horeson thore
And wyth a roke he smote hym sore:
On the hedde he brake the crowne,
That the blode faste ranne downe.
'Syr, thou doyst me dyshonowre,'
To Sowdan seyde Fabowre,
'When thou haste brokyn my heuedde.
The grace of god be fro me reuedde,
Yf thou were not my lordys sone,
Thou schuldyst abye, that thou haste done.'
Then seyde Sowdan: 'what seyeste thou?
Hast thou me manest nowe?
In evyll tyme thou hyt thoght:
Thyn own dethe thou haste wroght.'
And wyth his fyste he wolde hym smyte,
But Faber thoght hyt dyspyte:
On hys fete dud he stonde
And toke the chekur in hys honde.
He smote Sowdan undur the ere:
He felle to grounde and dyed there.

ANONYMOUS (15th century)

from *The Romance of Guy of Warwick*, lines 7511–7532

clepyd] *called*   thore] *then*   reuedde] *wrested*   abye] *pay for*   manest] *threaten*
despyte] *to deny*   chekur] *chessboard*

Falling Out

THE DUKE OF SESSE:
It was my chance one day to play at chess
For some few crowns, with a minion of this King's,
A mean poor man, that only served his pleasures;
Removing of a rook, we grew to words;
From this to hotter anger: to be short,
I got a blow. . . .

FRANCIS BEAUMONT AND JOHN FLETCHER

from *The Double Marriage*, II. I. 94–99

Epitaph for Capablanca

Now rests a mind as keen,
    A vision bright and clear,
As any that has been.
    And who is it lies here?

One that, erstwhile, no less
    Than Hindenburg could plan,
But played his game of chess
    And did no harm to man.

LORD DUNSANY

Duel in the Park

When did these grey ones
select this sagging bench
on which to balance their chess-board?

Did anyone see them come?
Are they the same two
who were here last year?

Black moves . . . shadow
of predatory fingers
poise above the White Queen.

Sun hovers low over taut
shoulders. Perambulator
and poodle depart.

A small squirrel surveys
possibilities.
Lovers linger. Silence stiffens.

Pawns are taken. A Knight exchanged
for a Bishop. Onlookers drift off,
others take their places.

When did the game start? Will it end soon?
Are these the same men
who played here last year?

LISA GRENELLE

The Chess Player

At last with stubborn jabs of your fingers
you kill the red cigarette bulb in the china dish;
expiring spirals of smoke
crinkle like lamb's fleece toward the ceiling,
and encumber the knights and bishops
on the chessboard, who hold their positions –
stupefied. Smoke-ring after smoke-ring snakes upward,
more agile than the gold mines on your fingers.

A window opens. One puff is enough
to panic the smoke's heaven-flung mirage
of imperial arches and battlements; –
down below another world moves:
a man, bruised by the sores of the wolf,
ignores your incense:
all the torture and formulae
of your small, heraldic, chessboard world.

For a time, I doubted if you yourself even
made any sense of the game, its square,
hobbled moves through gunpowder
clouds of tobacco . . . Poise cannot
pay off the folly of death; the flash
of your eyes asks that an answering crash
pierce the smoke-screen
thrown up by the god of chance to befriend you.

Today, I know what you want. I hear
the hoarse bell of the feudal campanile.
The archaic ivory chessmen are terrified.
Like snowmen, they melt in your mind's white glare.

ROBERT LOWELL

after *Nuove Stanze* by EUGENIO MONTALE (1896–1981)

The Winner

I had the talent before I played the game;
I made the black moves, then the white moves,
I just muled through whole matches with myself –
it wasn't too social only mating myself. . . .
But this guy in West Berlin whispers a move in my ear,
or there's a guy with his head right over my board –
they weren't too communicative with high chess.
Are most of your friends from the chess world?
I have a few peripheral friends here and there
who are non-chess players, but it's strange,
if you start partying around, it doesn't go.
I try to broaden myself, I read the racetrack,
but it's a problem if you lose touch with life . . .
because they want two world leaders to fight it out hand to hand.

R OBERT L OWELL

Check

My move, Sir? Oh, I am sorry, I thought it was yours.
To tell you the truth, my attention is somewhat shaken
When I think of so much I have lost for so little cause –
And worse, the things I missed that I might have taken.

I am depressed, when I look around at the board,
To see your predominance over my shrunken forces,
To see my land, which was once so deep and broad,
Domineered by your castles and prancing pitiless horses.

Your bishops are gone, it is true, for somehow I found
Their oblique advances not terribly hard to predict.
But the military promptly got control of the ground,
And threaten me worse. Frankly, I think I am licked.

I have to admit, with shame, that what ditched me was
My unkingly devotion to a madcap pawn.
I lived only for him: but he fell in an ambush, because
They forbade me to die for him. Now I live forlorn.

Is it worth fighting on? I am rather inclined to doubt it.
But strategy grows to a habit as douce as drink,
And the fact is, I should be terribly lost without it –
And what I should put in its place, I hate to think.

So have at you, Sir, in a modified sort of way.
Absurd to pretend that I relish the thought of dying,
But I mean not to sweat; and if you should trap me today
I shall yield with grace. After all, I was really not trying.

JOHN HOLMSTROM

Lord Dunsany

When I was thirteen years of age
In Lord Dunsany's House
We sat down at the chess board
And played at Cat and Mouse.

He seemed a wise old gentle man
With a pointed silver beard
But when the end game was begun
He spoke as I had feared.

'You have some knowledge of the play
And move the pieces well
But on the thirteenth move from now
I'll have you in my spell.'

Twelve moves went by, they seemed like hours,
I doubted what he said.
But when the thirteenth move was played
I found my King was dead.

MARCUS CUMBERLEGE

Chess Players

They sit in well-lit rows,
cufflinks sparkling over each battlefield
like stars. Is this what God was doing
at Flanders, Stalingrad?

The wooden men click. They're not fooled
by generals bargaining at tables.
They face each other. They die.
Spaces split slowly open like craters, wounds.

The women are somewhere else,
harmless, beyond hope.
In here is a perfect celibacy
– knights without favours, castles bare of maidens.

Sometimes it ends in madness
– Steinitz challenging that
star-sleeved General to match His mere omniscience
against the mind of a chessplayer.

Time shrivels like an ageing pianist's fingers
on keys where there are more harmonics
than atoms in the universe.
Yet nothing really happens

among these clocks and lights.
The end is a scarcity,
winds howling over the chequered plains.
Imagine moving words

like platoons into their slaughter
– you'd never get literature!
Yet the chessplayers talk of beauty.
Sometimes they sigh like lovers.

CAROL RUMENS

A Poem for Chessmen at a Congress

Shah maat — the King is dead

It's like an examination
– or some vast dinner party
where the guests sit in pairs
and politely demolish each other.
Your ranks of hunted shoulders
and frowns attest the passion
of the quest. For you are unravelling
a childhood, inching back.
You cross the polite, hushed street
– its pawn cars in a line,
its mitred evergreens –
and softly click the latches
to the room where the grown-ups stand
as if they'd guessed you'd visit
with death in your childish hand.
It's never enough, is it?
However well you win,
however bold your cry
of 'Checkmate, *Shah maat!*'
King Dad will rise again,
his crown unspilled, his lady
hard-faced at his side.
You mustn't think I'm gloating,
nor shiver when you hear
the whispering of my skirts
along the aisles where those
dumb beasts, the backs of your heads,
graze in their sensual doze.
I'm miles from the queening square.
Although no doubt in time,
we will change places,
for now you needn't run.

My history is not yours.
Long ago, I set up my pieces
against my father, as you did,
but it was only for fun.
Pretty face, I was free to lose.

CAROL RUMENS

3   *Philosophies*

False Fortune

My boldnesse ys turned to shame,
For fals Fortune hath pleyd a game
Atte ches with me, allas the while!
The trayteresse fals and ful of gyle, . . .
At the ches with me she gan to pleye;
With her false draughtes dyvers
She staal on me, and tok my fers.
And whan I sawgh my fers awaye,
Allas! I kouthe no lenger playe,
But seyde, 'Farewel, swete, ywys,
And farewel al that ever ther ys!'
Therwith Fortune seyde 'Chek her!'
And 'Mat!' in myd poynt of the chekker,
With a poun errant, allas!
Ful craftier to pley she was
Than Athalus, that made the game
First of the ches, so was hys name.
But God wolde I had oones or twyes
Ykoud and knowe the jeupardyes
That kowde the Grek Pithagores!
And kept my fers the bet therby.
And thogh wherto? for trewely
I hold that wyssh nat worth a stree!
Hyt had be never the bet for me.
For Fortune kan so many a wyle,
Ther be but fewe kan hir begile,
And eke she ys the lasse to blame;
Myself I wolde have do the same,
Before God, hadde I ben as she;
She oghte the more excused be.

draughtes] *moves at chess*   fers] *counsellor; the chess piece in Chaucer's period*
becoming known also as the queen, and here apparently so regarded   kouthe] *was able*
to   poun] *pawn*   ykoud] *understood*   kowde] *knew, understood*   the bet] *the*
better   stree] *straw*   kan] *knows, understands*   kan] *know how to, are able to*
lasse] *less*

For this I say yet more therto,
Had I be God and myghte have do
My wille, whan she my fers kaughte,
I wolde have drawe·the same draughte.
For, also wys God yive me reste,
I dar wel swere she took the beste.
But through that draughte I have lorn
My blysse; allas! that I was born!

GEOFFREY CHAUCER

from *The Book of the Duchess*, lines 617–620, 652–686

drawe] *moved*

from Destiny

Strange and unnatural! Let's stay and see
    This pageant of a prodigy.
Lo, of themselves the enlivened chessmen move,
Lo, the unbred, ill-organed pieces prove
    As full of art and industry,
    Of courage and of policy,
As we ourselves who think there's nothing wise but we.
    Here a proud Pawn I admire
    That still advancing higher
    At top of all became
    Another thing and name.
Here I'm amazed at the actions of a Knight,
    That does bold wonders in the fight.
    Here I the losing party blame
    For those false moves that break the game,
That to their grave, the bag, the conquered pieces bring
And above all, the ill conduct of the mated King.

Whate'er these seem, whate'er philosophy
    And sense or reason tell (said I)
These things have life, election, liberty;
    'Tis their own wisdom moulds their state,
    Their faults and virtues make their fate.
    They do, they do (said I) but strait
Lo from my enlightened eyes the mists and shadows fell
That hinder spirits from being visible.
And, lo, I saw two Angels played the mate.
With man, alas, no otherwise it proves,
    An unseen hand makes all their moves.
    And some are great, and some are small,
Some climb to good, some from good fortune fall,
    Some wise men, and some fools we call,
Figures, alas, of speech, for Destiny plays us all. . . .

ABRAHAM COWLEY

The Chequer-Board

'Tis all a Chequer-board of Nights and Days
Where Destiny with Men for Pieces plays:
Hither and thither moves, and mates, and slays,
And one by one back in the Closet lays.

EDWARD FITZGERALD

from *Rubáiyát of Omar Khayyám* (1st edition)

from Time and the Witch Vivien

VIVIEN   I lose! They're loaded dice. Time always plays
With loaded dice. Another chance! Come, father;
Come to the chess, for young girls' wits are better
Than old men's any day, as Merlin found.
                    [*Places the chess-board on her knees.*
The passing of those little grains is snow
Upon my soul, old Time.
                    [*She lays the hour-glass on its side.*
TIME   No; thus it stands.   [*Rights it again.*
For other stakes we play. You lost the glass.

VIVIEN   Then give me triumph in my many plots.
TIME   Defeat is death.
VIVIEN   Should my plots fail I'd die.   [*They play.*
   Thus play we first with pawns, poor things and weak;
   And then the great ones come, and last the king.
   So men in life and I in magic play;
   First dreams, and goblins, and the lesser sprites,
   And now with Father Time I'm face to face.

                                          [*They play.*

   I trap you.
TIME   Check.
VIVIEN   I do miscalculate.
   I am dull today, or you were now all lost.
   Chance, and not skill, has favoured you, old father!

                                          [*She plays.*

TIME   Check.
VIVIEN   Ah! how bright your eyes. How swift your moves.
   How still it is! I hear the carp go splash,
   And now and then a bubble rise. I hear
   A bird walk on the doorstep.   [*She plays.*
TIME   Check once more.
VIVIEN   I must be careful now. I have such plots –
   Such war plots, peace plots, love plots – every side;
   I cannot go into the bloodless land
   Among the whimpering ghosts.
TIME   Mate thus.
VIVIEN   Already?
   Chance hath a skill!   [*She dies.*

   W. B. YEATS

Atherton's Gambit

The master played the bishop's pawn,
For jest, while Atherton looked on;
The master played this way and that,
And Atherton, amazed thereat,
Said 'Now I have a thing in view
That will enlighten one or two,
And make a difference or so
In what it is they do not know.'

The morning stars together sang
And forth a mighty music rang –
Not heard by many, save as told
Again through magic manifold
By such a few as have to play
For others, in the Master's way,
The music that the Master made
When all the morning stars obeyed.

Atherton played the bishop's pawn
While more than one or two looked on;
Atherton played this way and that,
And many a friend, amused thereat,
Went on about his business
Nor cared for Atherton the less;
A few stood longer by the game,
With Atherton to them the same.

The morning stars are singing still,
To crown, to challenge, and to kill;
And if perforce there falls a voice
On pious ears that have no choice
Except to urge an erring hand
To wreak its homage on the land,
Who of us that is worth his while
Will, if he listen, more than smile?

Who of us, being what he is,
May scoff at others' ecstasies?
However we may shine today,
More-shining ones are on the way;
And so it were not wholly well
To be at odds with Azrael, –
Nor were it kind of any one
To sing the end of Atherton.

EDWIN ARLINGTON ROBINSON

Dust of Taken Pieces

So the four souls are ranged, the chess-board set.
The dark, invisible hand of secret Fate
Brought it to come to being that they met
After so many years of lying in wait.
While we least think it he prepares his Mate.
Mate, and the King's pawn played, it never ceases,
Though all the earth is dust of taken pieces.

JOHN MASEFIELD

from 'The Widow in the Bye Street', lines 162–168

Chess

Two Gods devise the scene:
White moves, and Black replies:
a bishop squints malignly at a queen:
a knight theatrically leaps between:
a hopeful pawn plods out and sharply dies:
the stolid castles guard the cowering kings:
two Gods watch all, like hawks on wakeful wings.

Two Gods alone contend:
they fight with mental beams
more keen than flame, more obdurate than rock.
Two wrestling twists of thought-stuff interlock:
two struggling patterns meet, but never blend:
strict thrusting rays now threaten, now defend:
mesh-like ideas make war on lacy dreams.
Meanwhile the troubled puppets in the squares
see not the sole significance which is theirs.

JOHN THOMPSON

Play

Your move I would have
said, but he was not
playing; my game a dilemma
that was without horns.

As though one can sit at table
with God! His mind shines
on the black and the white
squares. We stake our all

on the capture of the one
queen, as though to hold life
to ransom. He, if he plays, plays
unconcernedly among the pawns.

R. S. THOMAS

Chess-Men

A sad air of enforced tranquillity
surrounds their rigid world, in which they move
so circumscribed that every hour must prove
their virtuous and grave nobility.

The moves change, but the scene is as before;
mourners and mourned live out their endless life
in classic silence and conditioned strife,
exposed on the arena's parquet floor.

What is the plan, and whose manoeuvres these,
where friends are enemies, enemies friends?
If this is battle, why then are the ends
bloodless defeats and bloodless victories?

Both ivory and ebony are made
without the sense of weaker and of stronger:
these symbols and their kingdoms are no longer
the headstrong players, but the passive played.

Their lives lack meaning, yet the strategy
by which their blinded footsteps are constrained
they dimly sense, and long to have explained.
And while they wait, the dual deity

whose hands reach down as from a distant throne
lets fall into the armies' waiting ear
occasional hints of strife in his own sphere,
of fiercer battles, which he fights alone.

R. H. MORRISON

Idea

Idea blazes in darkness, a lonely star.
The witching hour is not twelve, but one.
Pure thought, in principle, some say, is near
Madness, but the independent mind thinks on,
Breathing and burning, abstract as the air.

Supposing all this were a game of chess.
One learned to do without the pieces first,
And then the board; and finally, I guess,
Without the game. The lightship gone adrift,
Endangering others with its own distress.

O holy light! All other stars are gone,
The shapeless constellations sag and fall
Till navigation fails, though ships go on
This merry, mad adventure as before
Their single-minded masters meant to drown.

HOWARD NEMEROV

The Perseus Chess

Time. Time for another move
In the slow intricate chess of my poetry.
Time, and another attempt at the Perseus poem
Abandoned a year ago. A year to the day.
– Imperceptible changes in the geology
Of the monstrous land. Rock forming and eroding.

My mind uneasy how to manipulate the pieces
To combine the disparate powers. Perseus,
Hot words written in his helmed killer's brain,
Who must bring the unfindable, the demanded
The undesired tribute to the complacent king:
Her head, Medusa's, her petrifying, serpent-rhythmed head.

My hand stretches out, waits, then lifts
The warrior-piece, places it forward one pace
Among the stone, the weathered effigies
Who creature the landscape. Check. One more
Move made. The leaden pulse of the sea sounds
In the ammonite ears of the pre-Jurassic men.

GERARD BENSON

4 Moralities

Both Check and Mate

He that is bothe chek and mate
   It is full hevy to restore;
Whan al is go it is to late
   To weshe and wepe after more.
Than be Avysed well before,
   That the fyrst draughte be weel drawe,
For whan the game is lore
   Thy part is not worthe an hawe.

ANONYMOUS (15th century)

from 'Good Rule is Out of Remembrance', lines 81–88

go] *gone*   draughte] *move*   drawe] *played*   lore] *lost*   hawe] *haw, fruit of the hawthorn*

A Game at Chess: Prologue

What of the game called chess-play can be made
To make a stage-play shall this day be played.
First you shall see the men in order set,
States and their Pawns, when both the sides are met,
The Houses well distinguished; in the game
Some men entrapped and taken, to their shame,
Rewarded by their play. And in the close
You shall see check-mate given to virtue's foes.
But the fairest jewel that our hopes can deck
Is so to play our game to avoid your check.

THOMAS MIDDLETON

The Man that Hath No Love of Chess

The man that hath no love of chess
    Is, sooth to say, a sorry wight,
Disloyal to his King and Queen,
    A faithless and ungallant Knight.
He hateth our good Mother Church
    And sneereth at the Bishop's lawn.
May Fortune check him till he hath
    His Castles and estates in Pawn.

    ANONYMOUS (18th century)

A Pawn's a Pawn for A' That

A Pawn's a Pawn for a' that,
    A wee bit Pawn an' a' that.
The Pawn that wins the farthest square
    Shall rule the day for a' that.

The muckle pieces come and gang.
    The Pawn gangs on for a' that.
He never fears the thickest thrang;
    But stan's or fa's for a' that.

D'ye see yon birky ca'd a Knicht,
　　Hits twa at once an' a' that.
A canny Pawn gies him a fricht
　　An' back he flees for a' that.

An' there the Bishop wi' a rush
　　Springs at the King an' a' that.
The Pawns together forward push
　　An' beat him back for a' that.

An' weel I ken a swaggerin' loon
　　They ca' a Rook an' a' that.
A Pawn may bring the fellow doon
　　An' kick him oot for a' that.

An' lo! the bonny Queen, hersel'
　　Worth twa big Rooks an' a' that.
A wee bit chancy Pawn may sell
　　An' trip her up for a' that.

The King, who proodly tak's his staun',
　　His guards aroon an' a' that,
Yields no' that seldom to a Pawn
　　Who cries 'Checkmate' for a' that.

A Pawn can mak' a belted Knicht,
　　A Bishop, Rook an' a' that;
A Queen is no' abune his micht.
　　Guid faith! he'll even fa' that.

W. Cook Spens

Chess

At the penultimate move, their saga nearly sung,
They have worked so hard to prove what lads they were when young,
Have looked up every word in order to be able to say
The gay address unheard when they were dumb and gay.
Your Castle to King's Fourth under your practised hand!
What is the practice worth, so few being left to stand?
Better the raw levies jostling in the square
Than two old men in a crevice sniping at empty air;
The veterans on the pavement puff their cheeks and blow
The music of enslavement that echoes back 'I told you so';
The chapped hands fumble flutes, the tattered posters cry
Their craving for recruits who have not had time to die.
While our armies differ they move and feel the sun,
The victor is a cypher once the war is won.
Choose your gambit, vary the tactics of your game,
You move in a closed ambit that always ends the same.

LOUIS MACNEICE

Chess

He sits all day and plays his game of chess.
Alone – a champion of retirement.
This round is won, this last decade of sums
Shrinking his time into a silent square.

He knows he is the master of success
After those years of metal, hooks and knives
That stiffened fingers, shrunk his bones, his neck,
Clawing his days into a spine of care.

He wears a mandarin's impassiveness.
But now – for a most concentrating move:
His eyes are sharper and his Queen secure –
'Check Mate' he roars across the empty chair.

LOTTE KRAMER

Checkmate

Queen The crown is haggard on my October hair.
  My gold robes stand apart from me like sheaves,
  And I shall bear no other summer, mortal
  To harvest, now that the utmost grapes have narrowed
  Irrevocably into wine, and the last leaves
  Have shaken from me who was white once
  And full as a cherry tree. The bitter sun
  Has ripened me till, expert past all caring,
  I walk the swept streets in my dry wisdom
  I who wept and fell in the rain of spring.

Knight Geometrically I have ridden away
  From the last highway on the clock, and now
  I come to the dark cul-de-sac of time.
  I shall not move again. There waits a finger
  On the lock of every hill to bar the pass
  And every track is blind with stone. The birds,
  Valiant in flight, have left my quiet banner
  That moves with the mist as though already ghost.
  My spurs glimmer deep down, like fish that flash
  And live in a universe I cannot breathe.

Rook Toppling through a quick fluster of waves
  Out of the harsh and smooth, the dark and white,
  I have gained veritable water where the sea
  In deepest patience holds me overwhelmed.
  I found no comfort in the stone my strength
  And have no shelter now to give, profoundly
  Gone out of the scuttling air that claws
  At bold humanity. High up above
  A bell still rings where once my tower was,
  Lolling on the tide to tell of a new danger.

Bishop It was all ceremonial. Singing processions
Swayed through the veins of the cathedral,
I at the heart of it, I at the altar.
My own sure breath swinging like a censer.
But allegory dies, and incense clouds
No mirror now. My brilliant book of hours
Shone like a peacock's tail, and all my saints
Are a white window. Hollow the candle flames
Echo a noon sung long since. I kneel
Shadowless, and vulnerable even so.

King Kings may be pawns, but royal is still a word
With Pharaoh in it, and rock, and stormy trumpets
That bluster through the crevices of time.
I am defeated, but at last I know
This kingly truth: the palm of a hand was all
My father saw, and all that I shall ever
See, until the hand throws down its law
And government rolls to the foot of the world,
Until the age-long game is folded up
In darkness, and the sky unclasps the sun.

PATRICIA BEER

A Game of Chess

The quiet moves, the gently shaded room:
It is like childhood once again when I
Sat with a tray of toys and you would come
To take my temperature and make me lie
Under the clothes and sleep. Now peacefully

We sit above the intellectual game.
Pure mathematics seems to rule the board
Emotionless. And yet I feel the same
As when I sat and played without a word
Inventing kingdoms where great feelings stirred.

Is it that knight and king and small squat castle
Store up emotion, bringing it under rule,
So that the problems now with which we wrestle
Seem simply of the mind? Do feelings cool
Beneath the order of an abstract school?

Never entirely, since the whole thing brings
Me back to childhood when I was distressed:
You seem the same who put away my things
At night, my toys and tools of childish lust.
My king is caught now in a world of trust.

ELIZABETH JENNINGS

The Game's the Thing

for David Jenkins, who knows Boppo well

When Boppo played the chess cafés of Montevideo
it was all King's Gambit stuff, sacrificial attacks
on the castled opponent, pawns scattered over the board.
Boppo threw away bishops like someone who hated the clergy.
'I'm a chess-player in a world of draughts!' he cried.
But wait – in more serious games, all too often
not '!', '?', but '?!' . . . 'Original but unsound'. . .
would be the appropriate annotation. Still,
perhaps this time, Boppo – now punching the air
like a footballer scoring: 'You're on Red Taffy Alert!'
The opponent shrivels, and Boppo pours one more wine.
Five minutes later an ear-splitting 'I've blown it!'
Poor old Boppo! Why is it his wins don't equate with his talent?
'Still, if I lose, I at least lose memorably' –
and shrewdly, 'As well that I'm not a mountaineer.'
Yet, if things reach a really tight endgame
Boppo becomes a precisian of keen calculation,
nursing each tiny advantage; no Taffy-play now
but for one last wriggle: the draw by perpetual check.

ANDREW WATERMAN

from 'The Tasserty File'

Pawn

So, I go forward, mud clogging my boots.
I might as well be back behind my plough,
Hunger scraping my belly. I sailed away
For a shilling and a feather in my hat.
The smoke of my breath is smothered in mist;
I am walking into a witch's clouded glass.
I have carried this war too long on my back.
If I had the courage, I would throw it down and run.
I sing between my teeth, nail down the rhymes of my song:

God rot the bloody sergeant
    And his snarling drum
That drove me into a foreign land,
    And I wish I was home.

He took me into a tavern,
    Brown ale he bought for me,
And I promised him my right arm
    In the name of liberty.

God strike that devil the sergeant,
    A white shilling he gave to me,
And I sold him my red heart's blood,
    And I wish I was free.

Out of the mist, between the birch trees,
A man walks, the mud clogs his boots,
Armour like mine, but red where mine is white.
In his own language, he sings between his teeth.
I wish I could tell if his song was like mine.
He lifts up his open hand. I can see him smile.
In this wilderness, nobody watches.
I smile slowly, lift my open hand.

JOY RUTHERFORD

A Game of Chess

in memory of C. H. O'D. Alexander

Plot and counterplot, maze
of possible lines, threads
to unravel, silent
conspiracies: my brain
reels, there is no certain
path. Abortive attack,
likely defences, ebb
and flow – if this, but that
then this; combinations
surfacing in the web
of thought, half-seen. Beyond
the calculable, one
prays for deliverance
from evil. Wait; then push
the pawn forward, hoping.

PETER JAY

Life of the Pawn

to Ştefan Aug. Doinaş
'les Pions . . . sont l'âme des Echecs' – PHILIDOR

Forward at first – two steps.
Then more cautiously, one
pace only when protected. Now
the time comes to resist, facing
attack from every angle.
We may too recklessly take up
a forward, exposed position,
or under restraint behave
too timidly. Nevertheless
we have strength in numbers,
we have to be closely watched.
The majority of us accept
passive roles; motionless
we may appear to be, but
we give each other support.
Though we can never retreat
we know how to stand still.
We capture deviously.
      Sometimes
we are sacrificed in a cause,
not knowing precisely why;
for us, in general, the game's
the thing, since we know the outcome
is usually decided by other
stronger forces. More often though
we are lost in desperation
or simply abandoned, picked off.

But we have aspirations. Clear
our paths and on we press –
step by step creating
delicate shifts in the balance
of power. Not threatening

in ourselves, we can seem
to threaten to become threats
that cannot be dealt with.

In the end just one of us can
be enough to decide everything.

PETER JAY

5 *Public Worlds*

For Ye Play So

For ye play so at the chess,
As they suppose and guess,
That some of you but late
Hath played so checkmate
With lords of great estate
After such a rate,
That they shall mell nor make,
Nor upon them take,
For king nor kayser sake,
But at the pleasure of one
That ruleth the roost alone.

JOHN SKELTON

from *Collyn Clout*, lines 1010—1020

mell] *mingle, interfere*   make] *do, act*

from Becket

PROLOGUE

A Castle in Normandy. Interior of the Hall. Roofs of a City seen thro'
Windows.

HENRY and BECKET at chess.

HENRY   So then our good Archbishop Theobald
   Lies dying.
BECKET   I am grieved to know as much.
HENRY   But we must have a mightier man than he
   For his successor.
BECKET   Have you thought of one?

HENRY A cleric lately poisoned his own mother,
   And being brought before the courts of the Church,
   They but degraded him. I hope they whipped him.
   I would have hanged him.
BECKET   It is your move.
HENRY Well – there.   [*Moves.*
   The Church in the pell-mell of Stephen's time
   Hath climbed the throne and almost clutched the crown;
   But by the royal customs of our realm
   The Church should hold her baronies of me,
   Like other lords amenable to law.
   I'll have them written down and made the law.
BECKET My liege, I move my Bishop.
HENRY   And if I live,
   No man without my leave shall excommunicate
   My tenants or my household.
BECKET   Look to your King.
HENRY No man without my leave shall cross the seas
   To set the Pope against me – I pray your pardon.
BECKET Well – will you move?
HENRY   There then!   [*Moves.*
BECKET Why – there then, for you see my Bishop
   Hath brought your King to a standstill. You are beaten.
HENRY   [*Kicks over the board.*
   Why, there then – down go Bishop and King together.
   I loathe being beaten; had I fixed my fancy
   Upon the game I would have beaten thee.

ALFRED, LORD TENNYSON

Chesspieces

It was a time of trouble – executions,
Dearth, searches, nightly firing, balked escapes –
And I sat silent, while my cellmate figured
Ruy Lopez' Gambit from the 'Praxis'. Silence
Best fitted with our mood: we seldom spoke.
'I have a thought,' he said, tilting his stool.
'We prisoners are so many pieces taken,
Swept from the board, only used again
When a new game is started.' 'There's that hope,'
I said, 'the hope of being used again.
Some day of strength, when ploughs are out in March,
The Dogs of Fionn will slip their iron chains,
And, heedless of torn wounds and failing wind,
Will run the old grey Wolf to death at last.'
He smiled, 'I like the image. My fat Kings
And painted Queens, and purple-cassocked Bishops
Are tame, indeed, beside your angry Dogs!'

JOSEPH CAMPBELL

Before Gunpowder

At chess, before gunpowder,
The Queen took only
Diagonal steps.

W. H. AUDEN

from 'Symmetries and Asymmetries'

Another Cold May

With heads like chessmen, bishop or queen,
The tulips tug at their roots and mourn
In inaudible frequencies, the move
Is the wind's, not theirs; fender to fender
The cars will never emerge, not even
Should their owners emerge to claim them, the move
Is time's, not theirs; elbow to elbow
Inside the roadhouse drinks are raised
And downed, and downed, the pawns and drains
Are blocked, are choked, the move is nil,
The lounge is, like the carpark, full,
The tulips also feel the chill
And tilting leeward do no more
Than mimic a bishop's move, the square
Ahead remains ahead, their petals
Will merely fall and choke the drains
Which will be all; this month remains
False animation of failed levitation,
The move is time's, the loss is ours.

LOUIS MACNEICE

The Moon and the Night and the Men

On the night of the Belgian surrender the moon rose
Late, a delayed moon, and a violent moon
For the English or the American beholder;
The French beholder. It was a cold night,
People put on their wraps, the troops were cold
No doubt, despite the calendar, no doubt
Numbers of refugees coughed, and the sight
Or sound of some killed others. A cold night.

On Outer Drive there was an accident:
A stupid well-intentioned man turned sharp
Right and abruptly he became an angel
Fingering an unfamiliar harp,
Or screamed in hell, or was nothing at all.
Do not imagine this is unimportant.
He was a part of the night, part of the land,
Part of the bitter and exhausted ground
Out of which memory grows.

                       Michael and I
Stared at each other over chess, and spoke
As little as possible, and drank and played.
The chessmen caught in the European eye,
Neither of us I think had a free look
Although the game was fair. The move one made
It was difficult at last to keep one's mind on.
'. . . hurt and unhappy' said the man in London.
We said to each other, The time is coming near
When none shall have books or music, none his dear,
And only a fool will speak aloud his mind.
History is approaching a speechless end,
As Henry Adams said. Adams was right.

All this occurred on the night when Leopold
Fulfilled the treachery four years before

Begun – or was he well-intentioned, more
Roadmaker to hell than king? At any rate,
The moon came up late and the night was cold,
Many men died – although we know the fate
Of none, nor of anyone, and the war
Goes on, and the moon in the breast of man is cold.

JOHN BERRYMAN

Playing Through Old Games of Chess

A crane-fly trembles in the windowpane
as it has since before there were windows . . .
I play through old games of chess: their rich diapason
a blossoming in the room, as of huge heavy-headed roses.

Outside, the hottest summer since records began,
and the traffic-lights signalling insane morse,
a jabber of red green amber, somewhere a computer
has overheated, fouling the traffic and tempers

are overheated, and all along the Thames
the bridges shove themselves over from metal expansion.
Ah, the ecologists say, it is carbon dioxide
irreversibly building up in the upper atmosphere

due to industrial waste, and all kinds of waste
accumulate irreversibly, and we record it,
even the mineral ores of language processed through
to a standing slag beyond recycling;

and economists say it is the economy overheated.
The plane trees shimmer through rising petrol fumes,
and children's voices ascend to tinkle against the bowl
of a blue sky hazed with entropy, our last heat-death.

I reset the pieces and start again:
Steinitz versus Tchigorin, Ruy Lopez, Morphy Defence,
Havana, 1892, and decorously
the opposite knights step forth, the kings are castled to safety

for a while. And still for a while
beyond the cities in meadows (but a hum of traffic hanging)
the cows, as then, stand four-square over their shadows,
while one by one white petals slip into sun-dappled water

to float, for a while; and the woods are dark with summer,
greenness sloping to greenness to a far
horizon marked with the faint stroke of a steeple
as it has been since before there were

– steeples, I almost said. At least as when
all history seemed a sort of sunlit incline upwards,
with problems like the Balkans, abolishing cholera, crime,
certainly soluble, and change meant improvement,

hygiene, gas cooking, fast travel, the bioscope.
Beneath 'Truman, Hanbury, Buxton & Comps. Entire'
the old photograph shows clay pipes and boaters around an ale-
        bench,
and Spoonbeam is not out at lunch for Lancs for ever,

while at dusk, his cycle-lamp catching gold motes
along deep lanes where roots twist and convolvulus clings,
comes Cholmondeley to talk, over whiskey by leaded windows,
of *The Origin of Species* or *The Idylls of the King*.

The pawn-structure looks sound, across the board *andante*
the full orchestration unfolds, with recurring motifs and grace-notes,
rounding Good Hope the *Ariel* bringing home tea from China,
cablegrams under the sea, while in Afghan hill-posts

or where a delta's archipelagos of bamboo huts
coalesce to a port of old palaces, crumbling pagodas,
men with iron moustaches bat out their time
outstaring all sundowns from the verandah.

Of course, through the looking-glass all was different,
and moving forward got you nowhere, the miners
stonily piling their barrows after the latest eviction
cannot see their great-grandsons' Cortinas, package-tour fritterings,

and the husband who tendered with flowers the most honourable
        intentions
is hanging his stovepipe hat on the bedposts of whores;

and every life dark-edged, the hushed death-rooms, the infant graves;
and perhaps it is all the tinman's dream

who stationed at the street corner pedals his grinding-wheel
for ever. And as for the countless hordes
of Indians and Chinese, it is not their game
at all, they have nothing to learn but patience.

Exchange of queens: the general liquidation
which follows seems to favour White, a sacrificial
manoeuvre clinches things, for the while. If today
in Flanders the farmer again wades through barley where all nature

was murdered, still the old dynasts have toppled like chess-kings,
and however we go through the motions again
(the squares are being done up, houses wormy with their past
are scoured, the cellars blocked off as if there were bones down in
        them,

layers of cheap flowered paper torn from each wall),
or trace the lines not followed, unrealized combinations
in notes as much as the moves played part of the game,
the quality of that long, lost summer cannot be restored

— when June rang like a gong for Pax Britannica,
and Europe's chordage held the world enthralled;
and in London, St Petersburg, Vienna or Baden Baden
the old chess-masters' arias thrilled. Until Lasker, who

would research Relativity, talk with Einstein, flee
the Nazis, shifted a piece irrevocably changing
the chemistry of the game, its lovely architectonics;
while a crane-fly trembled in the windowpane.

ANDREW WATERMAN

6   *Personal Relations*

Checkmate

Now every man that ys alone,
That shuld be wedded to such a on,
I cownsayl hym rather to have non
    At the townys end.

Lest he be knokked abowt the pate;
Then to repent yt ys to late,
When on his cheke he ys chekmate
    At the townys end.

Anonymous (16th century)

from 'Strife in the House', lines 51–58

To the Lady that Scorned her Lover

Although I had a check,
To give the mate is hard.
For I have found a neck,
To keep my men in guard.
And you that hardy are
To give so great assay
Unto a man of war,
To drive his men away,

neck] *move to cover check*   assay] *test*

I rede you, take good heed,
And mark this foolish verse:
For I will so provide,
That I will have your ferse.
And when your ferse is had,
And all your war is done:
Then shall your self be glad
To end that you begun.
For if by chance I win
Your person in the field:
Too late then come you in
Your self to me to yield.
For I will use my power,
As captain full of might,
And such will I devour,
As use to show me spite.
    And for because you gave
Me check in such degree,
This vantage lo I have:
Now check, and guard to thee.
    Defend it, if thou may:
Stand stiff, in thine estate.
For sure I will assay,
If I can give thee mate.

HENRY HOWARD, EARL OF SURREY

rede] *advise*   ferse] *chess piece: 'counsellor' or queen*

from Women Beware Women

LIVIA   Alas, poor widow, I shall be too hard for thee.

MOTHER   Y'are cunning at the game, I'll be sworn, madam.

LIVIA   It will be found so, ere I give you over.
She that can place her man well –

MOTHER   As you do, madam.

LIVIA   As I shall, wench, can never lose her game.
Nay, nay, the black king's mine.

MOTHER   Cry you mercy, madam.

LIVIA   And this my queen.

MOTHER   I see't now.

LIVIA   Here's a duke
Will strike a sure stroke for the game anon –
Your pawn cannot come back to relieve itself.

MOTHER   I know that, madam.

LIVIA   You play well the whilst.
How she belies her skill! I hold two ducats
I give you check and mate to your white king,
Simplicity itself, your saintish king there.

MOTHER   Well, ere now lady
I have seen the fall of subtlety. Jest on.

LIVIA   Ay, but simplicity receives two for one.

MOTHER   What remedy but patience!

[*At this juncture is interposed a scene 'above' in which, as contrived by Livia, the Mother's innocent young daughter-in-law Bianca is seduced by the worldly Duke; apropos which the ongoing chess-game of course provides ironic commentary and symbolism. That in Jacobean times 'duke' was an alternative name for 'rook' is exploited in the dialogue.* – ED.]

LIVIA   Did I not say my duke would fetch you over, widow?

MOTHER   I think you spoke in earnest when you said it, madam.

LIVIA   And my black king makes all the haste he can too.

MOTHER   Well, madam, we may meet with him in time yet.

LIVIA   I have given thee blind mate twice.
MOTHER   You may see, madam.
    My eyes begin to fail.
LIVIA   I'll swear they do, wench.

THOMAS MIDDLETON

Act II Scene 2, lines 294–310, 388–393

from The Chess Master and His Fair Pupil

. . . Miss Browne and I set up the men,
    She a piano opening led;
    I felt a whirling in my head,
And in my heart a fluttering pain.

Her beauty had possessed my soul;
    I ne'er saw anything so fair;
    It almost drove me to despair,
And placed my thoughts beyond control.

She won, but most politely said
    I let her win, 'twas not her skill;
    Next I played with a steadier will,
And trod in stern Caissa's tread.

As time went on I calmer grew,
    And gave my lessons twice a week;
    Her Chess indeed, was very weak,
Much weaker than she ever knew. . . .

CHARLES TOMLINSON

My Liefest Lover

I speak, and longing love upties me and unties me;
Till with her honey-dew of inner lip she plies me:
I brought the chess-board and my liefest lover plays me
With white and black, but black-cum-white ne'er satisfies me:

'Twas as if King for Castle I were fain to place me
Till wilful loss of game atwixt two queens surprise me
And if I seek to read intent in eyes that eye me,
Oh man! that glance askance with hint of wish defies me.

RICHARD BURTON

translated from *Arabian Nights*

The Chess-Board

Irene, do you yet remember
Ere we were grown so sadly wise,
Those evenings in the bleak December,
Curtain'd warm from the snowy weather,
When you and I play'd chess together,
   Checkmated by each other's eyes?
   Ah, still I see your soft white hand
Hovering warm o'er Queen and Knight,
   Brave Pawns in valiant battle stand:
The double Castles guard the wings:
The Bishop, bent on distant things,
Moves, sidling, through the fight,
   Our fingers touch; our glances meet,
   And falter; falls your golden hair
   Against my cheek; your bosom sweet
Is heaving. Down the field, your Queen
Rides slow her soldiery all between,
   And checks me unaware.
   Ah me! the little battle's done,
Disperst is all its chivalry;
Full many a move, since then, have we
'Mid Life's perplexing chequers made,
And many a game with Fortune play'd, –
   What is it we have won?
   This, this at least – if this alone; –
That never, never, never more,
As in those old still nights of yore,
   (Ere we were grown so sadly wise)
   Can you and I shut out the skies,
Shut out the world, and wintry weather,
And, eyes exchanging warmth with eyes,
Play chess, as then we play'd, together!

E. R. BULWER LYTTON, EARL OF LYTTON

Rimbaud and Verlaine

Rimbaud and Verlaine, precious pair of poets,
Genius in both (but what is genius?) playing
Chess on a marble table at an inn
With chestnut blossom falling in blond beer
And on their hair and between knight and bishop –
Sunlight squared between them on the chess-board
Cirrus in heaven, and a squeal of music
Blown from the leathern door of Ste Sulpice –

Discussing, between moves, iamb and spondee
Anacoluthon and the open vowel
God the great peacock with his angel peacocks
And his dependent peacocks the bright stars:
Disputing too of fate as Plato loved it,
Or Sophocles, who hated and admired,
Or Socrates, who loved and was amused:

Verlaine puts down his pawn upon a leaf
And closes his long eyes, which are dishonest,
And says 'Rimbaud, there is one thing to do:

We must take rhetoric, and wring its neck! . . .'
Rimbaud considers gravely, moves his Queen;
And then removes himself to Timbuctoo.

And Verlaine dead, – with all his jades and mauves;
And Rimbaud dead in Marseilles with a vision,
His leg cut off, as once before his heart;
And all reported by a later lackey,
Whose virtue is his tardiness in time.

Let us describe the evening as it is: –
The stars disposed in heaven as they are:
Verlaine and Shakspere rotting, where they rot,
Rimbaud remembered, and too soon forgot;

Order in all things, logic in the dark;
Arrangement in the atom and the spark;
Time in the heart and sequence in the brain –

Such as destroyed Rimbaud and fooled Verlaine.
And let us then take godhead by the neck –

And strangle it, and with it, rhetoric.

Conrad Aiken

from 'Preludes for Memnon'

126

Shah Mat

(The king is dead)

'Knight to king bishop three', your quiet words
Across the polished table bring to me
With curt precision what in former times
Might end at daybreak on a frosty ground,

Or I have read as much. Each battlefield
Is like another: hand-wrought jousting lance,
A stretch of lawn, silk sheets, a surgery,
But none perhaps so ominous as these

Arrayed in formal challenge, rank and file.
Your painted smile and coloured finger-ends
Caress the symbols of the day's despair

And you advance with mock simplicity,
Which I admit, but there are other days –
'My move' I say, and sally forth to fight.

JOHN CAMPBELL-KEASE

Chess Piece

Of all the pieces that I've played
　　There's none like lovely Rita.
I love to play her opening
　　No gambit could be neater.

She is positionally strong
　　She knows the variations,
But most of all I like to see
　　Her pretty combinations.

I tried to fork her one black night
　　But I miscalculated;
She niftily unpinned herself
　　And thus she got me mated.

JEDEDIAH BARROW

Lost and Found

The knights on his first chess set were mounted
On horses with close-together eyes and narrow noses:
An amused look whichever way they faced.
One day, the set was not complete. A knight
Was lost; he played half-heartedly for thirty years
With a plastic pepperpot instead. She walked into his room
Eventually at forty-one, with a set smile
And amused eyes close together under her forehead.
She took a step, and turned aside, smiling.
Consequently, life could be played properly again.

ALAN BROWNJOHN

The Chess Lesson

for Chrissie King

e4 c5 – and our half-open game
bristles for each with two-edged subtleties.
Wryly I meditate your searching lines,

I who have crossed the sea, left you behind
where adults play out children's games
and beating through your house-wall from next door

'Road Runner' on the hi-fi, loud again
the 'What-do-you-think-of-that-you-guys' refrain . . .
'I will not chide,' you wrote, 'deserting me,

yet keep me constant in your heart and mind.'
Beginners' Chess, p. 1, out leaps your name:
'The game is ended when the king is lost.'

Another room now, other couch,
and other woman. Shelves rope-hung and heaped
with loose-coiled mooring rope . . . Give rope enough . . .

And she here musing 'Why not, between friends?
All friends would do as much, and some do more.
What game is worth it if you keep the score?' . . .

Her sleep ghost-billows through thin wall
where dawn highlights the ad. for Slumberland:
'Out the wrong side? Perhaps the bed is wrong' . . .

I contemplate some middle-game exchange
('Solutions reached in safe analysis
impress less than those found across the board'),

and still tired, press the button on my clock.
Outside, grey seas allow each seagull's long
diagonal. None yet has made a move.

   DAVID JENKINS

A Game of Chess

I'm told you play chess? His question
is impertinent; I am in
his house. He amends, offers as
defence a Sicilian wine
with a high Alekhine content.
From black and white speakers the slow
movement from *Giuoco Piano*
and the *Steinitz Variation*.

He's a restricted man, squared four
like a moon in a turning field;
contrives patterns, miasma through
a microscope; believes Newton
affects the balance of his balls.
We sit out manoeuvres, rankers
constrained by Christian armistice,
felons trapping a pregnant hare.

I'm in his house. There are gestures
to be made and sighs to exhale.
Not being friends I may not ash his
floors with the nails of my cigars.
Or joke with his wife (the lovely
Fegatella, who offers Knorr's
gnocchi as a starter). Nor may
I lock eyes on eyes, legs in bed.

Locock's counter-attack is called
if I'm to mate his pretty queen,
sneers the villain (piece excluded
from the modern game). While he talks
and she cooks, I count my replies
to his question, his pertinence.
Compromised Defence, perhaps, but
pawn to king four has worked before.

BARRY COLE

The Most Difficult Position

— Wer mit dem Leben spielt,
Kommt nie zurecht;
Wer sich nicht selbst befiehlt,
Bleibt immer ein Knecht.

GOETHE

1   STAUNTON PROLOGIZES (SPRING, 1858)

Now mind those papers with your pretty foot!
They may not seem in order, but they are:
The order of the mind at least, the mind
That stacks the evidence with faultless art.
Dead king. Wicked uncle. Mad prince. Queen
Unusually weak, ambiguous.
I speak now of the Bard. The trick's the same:
To link the salient facts organically.
You see my labours at their deepest here,
With analogues from Scandinavian myth
And penny fables. I'm too proud to tread
The pitons of the frozen commentators?
Fair charge, not true. They're harbingers, not rivals.
I map what they surmised and at a stroke
I free the ice-bound glacier of their text
Till all is moving river, warm and full.
That's Theobald you tread on, Whiter you clutch
As though to dub me silent to your service!
My dear, I'm sorry. Something in your look
Speaks of a small offence, and yet you smile
Despite yourself. I like to talk to you,
Rare visitor, as Gertrude will not talk,
Nor talked to Theobald nor Whiter neither,
Whom you may now put down. He cost me much
To find. What is it, dear? Is that the time?
Well, well, I see. Is dinner cold? I'm sorry.
A fruitful morning swollen to a day
And like to drop untasted. I've worked well

But work's a tyrant. My edition grows
An ogre's task, eating up time and life;
Truth's straws for spinning into gold,
An ogre's task without the lucky ring,
Though you, dear, are my ring, and golden too
To help me shift the straws, defeat the ogre.
    I saw you in the garden through the window
Reaching for roses. You sustain my labours
As the bright stream an oak that arches over.
Thought in your presence is a growing silence
That feeds invisibly upon my love.
(Pass me my cigars: you will not mind?
Thank you. It helps me to unwind my thoughts.)
I have been thinking for an hour on end
About the guilt (or innocence) of Gertrude
Who had no time for roses, and was weak.
Strange that the ivory there, the red and white,
How strange that in her realm of four and sixty
Small distinct dominions the queen
Is most powerful! Did Shakespeare play the game?
Undoubtedly. And missed his dinner too,
Writing his high and witty heroines
Whose power lay in their tongues. (Another match:
The leaf is unwilling to admit the fire.
Sit down, too, and be patient. I will come
To sift the prandial leavings soon enough.)
    Time tells all, backwards as well as forwards,
Turns stage to altar and the luscious hybrid,
Static in crystal vases, to a nomad;
Chequered applewood and trailing hems
To our nude parents; and the ivory *vierge*
There by your elbow to a Persian *firz*,
Proud Amazon to greybeard counsellor.
When my edition's done, I may find time
To write a paper on the piece's role,
Its history and curious change of sex.
Yes, it would please me to explore the case,
But time's my tyrant, as you know, my dear.
If I could queen my hours into years!

I have my public and my publishers
Hot on my neck; the endless correspondence,
Friendly analysis of my past games
With Anderssen (the gross presumption of it!),
Offers to play, requests for information,
The search for books; the endless annotation,
Feeding the *Illustrated London News*,
My all-devouring column; queries from Routledge,
Hints of the advance and long delay.
It never stops. Look at this letter here.
It came this morning. No, you didn't see it.
You had that letter from your Indian cousin
If you remember. The New Orleans Chess Club,
I quote: 'The undersigned committee has
The honour to invite you to our city
And there meet Mr Morphy in a chess match.'
(Do they think that I could take the boat tomorrow?)
'We see no valid reason why an exercise
So intellectual and ennobling is
Excluded from the generous rivalry
Found between the Old World and the New
In every branch of human industry.'
(Pompous asses!) 'It unfortunately happens
That serious family affairs prevent
Mr Morphy from entertaining, for the present,
The thought of visiting Europe.' (Mummy won't let him!)
'The amount of the stakes, on either side, to be
Five thousand dollars.' Five thousand dollars?
Really, my dear, it is intolerable.
Does the boy think that life all over Europe
Can grind to a halt merely to give him the pleasure
Of sitting and facing his elders and betters over
A Lilliputian army of carved ivory?
     You smile, do you? Am I unreasonable?
You think I should be gracious and consent?
That I am world champion and can afford to?
Am I world champion, then? Am I indeed?
Don't you imagine that Mrs Anderssen
Is saying just the same today to him

And over the very same letter? Oh yes, I know
That I was out of practice when he beat me,
The grinning schoolmaster from frozen Breslau!
'Poor Staunton was out of practice.' It was a mistake
And I shall not repeat it. I am a scholar
And my work comes first. Five thousand dollars!
Someone somewhere hopes to make some money!
Morphy's games are very pretty but
They will not bear the test of analysing.
(My cigar is out again.) He's just a child!
A child beginning a career of conquest!
More like Barnum and Bailey's three-ring circus
With General Tom Thumb and other wonders.
What does the drum beat and the billboard say?
That Morphy played in the cradle; scorned his books,
Guessing the gambits as Newton knew his Euclid,
By intuition; beat Löwenthal at thirteen
And Paulsen in New York last year; recites
Unfalteringly from his memory
The entire Civil Code of Louisiana,
And what not else? With such politeness too,
The newsmen marvelling: 'Mr Paulsen never
Makes an oversight; I sometimes do.'
A circus! Am I to put on greasepaint then
And tumble for the eager multitude?
Would you like me to? You think it important?
You see me as your valiant Perceval?
    Important? My dear, consider. Please don't mistake me.
The game of chess is supremely unimportant:
As, shall we say, a trellis of climbing roses
Watered and cut by a sweet and gloveless lady
(Now, now! Don't hide it! Give me your tender scratches
So I may make a handy sandwich of them.
There, hidden in mine and healed by love!
I thrive upon such spiritual dining.)
The game of chess is unimportant as
The exercise of dogs or whisker-wax,
Hot meat brought level in with steady wrists,
A letter from a cousin in Jodhpur

With talk of franchise and a sale-of-work.
You see? It neither does nor does not matter.
A rose is beautiful, the meat gets cold
Or eaten, the cousin relieves her loneliness,
The dogs are healthy. So is my moustache.
Thus the queen moves this way or that way, thus
She is sacrificed, no more or less a queen
Than that in stone and sepia, two removes
From the banality, work of the box
And chemicals and ineffable loyalty
Of the Jodhpur cousin. Don't take away your hand!
I'm not teasing. It's true. Don't you see?
I love it. It's delightful and it's moral.
Its mimic battles are engaged upon
For neither prize nor honour. It's a game
For Aristotle not for Perceval
So how should it be used for a career?
    I'll show you what I mean. We'll play together,
You and I, as lovers used to do
In Europe's maytime. Push the board between us.
It's white and red, a contest like the roses.
I'll give you knight and rook, and you begin.
Every little lathing sings of the stage
Now, doesn't it? You see the fascination.
The happy warrior pops out like a sparrow
Quick under the blossoming may and steady,
His head small and alert upon its ruff.
There on the lawn, you see one? He's pretending
The philopluvial bisexuals can
Escape him, one eye out for the dangerous rival.
A page or two, attendant on the king?
Slight and foppish? Yes, but watch that worm!
The throat moves. A glove's or fan's adjusted.
Some grand theme is broached. Do you hear the words?
No matter. The scene changes. Sir Something's bold
To make a broil, raise an old quarrel or
Concoct an accusation of a sort.
An old story. Anything will do.
Sir Other's at him, and the pages freeze,

136

Locked face to face. The Sirs are at a distance
But engaged. Is it the Quiet Game?
You have me waiting. Thorns' stigmata hover
Above the board. I'm in my heaven now.
It's an age-old theatre that nature knows
And mounts each year not thinking of expense.
Infinite shapes! Tautologies of flowers!
Is it the Quiet Game? You like the Scotch.
I'd wager for the Scotch, a safe good game.
Your eye is sparkling, though. You know that custom
Stales. In moves your bishop like a cruet!
Down to Knight Five: that gives it flavour, just
A taste of risk. But can you see it through?
I never like to play this opening
Named for the advice of Ruy Lopez
In his *Libro del Arte del Juego del Axedres*:
Too much decisiveness too early here
And larger birds, their beaks festooned with worms,
May fly to freedom from their ravening.
But still, you see the life of the thing. My point
Is that it *is* like life, supremely so,
And all the world's a stage. The entrances
And exits finely done. Above all, exits!
Bishops arraign the weak Plantagenet,
The queen has some ideas of her own,
The old knight blusters, humoured by a boy
Who is not ignorant of the eighth square.
Plantagenet retires into his castle,
The queen has executions to arrange,
The knight must go. Yes, going out is all.
So many ways of going, many deaths.
The beak stabs suddenly like this, my dear,
And look: I have your pawn here in my hand,
Bald as a baby and as helpless, too.
As helpless as a worm. So many ways:
The boast, the whimper and the silent prayer,
The brute resistance and the daring feint,
The outraged protest and the resignation,
Self-slaughter, sui-mate, the noble gesture.

So many ways, and Shakespeare knew them all.
I understand it, or at least I try to.
I've mastered what I can. I am respected.
It is the game I love and not success.
Five years ago I challenged any comer
And no one came, not even Anderssen.
Now comes this boy, this Morphy. Shall I wait
On him? I think not. Shall I jump to the challenge
Of a boy with the face of a young girl in her teens?
I decline. I have a significant position.
I am Howard Staunton. I believe that I am happy.
The sun is low and strikes across the lawn
As the birds begin to sing. One crimson petal
Falls from your excellent roses. Your move, my dear.

2   MORPHY PERSISTS (SUMMER AND AUTUMN, 1858)

Mother, you'll think I've not written before because I forgot to
Or maybe because in the end I only too well remember
Your tears at the quayside, your tears and your casual hurt
    exhortations,
Your tears at my firm uncancelled intention, your tears at my silence.
Yes, I remember it all and it seemed a fitting departure
For one who had vowed to defy such an elusive opponent.
Tears cover many regrets and emotion's a difficult subject,
Likely, I think, to defeat all but the most assiduous,
Likely to daunt any student with its impossible answers
To all the unknown questions. Ascribe a motive to weeping!
Might as well go to the Mississippi for a true confession
Or rifle the desert for clues to long-lost extravagant feelings.
Moisture flies up the offered cheek and the ducts receive it,
Kisses stagger back through the no-man's-land of volition
Quite unhurt, though dazed and shocked and totally useless.
The *Arabia* hoots for the very last time and the hawsers are slackened.
There in the mind the dubious orders, checked and rechecked,
Yield not the slightest clue towards their interpretation.
Mother, I ask you: just what do you think you are losing?
Is it a dutiful son, or is it the wealthy attorney

You hoped perhaps I'd become if I persevered with my studies?
Have you examined the terms of that familiar equation?
Where is the unknown factor, the one that you've cancelled out?
Wouldn't success in itself give a more satisfactory answer?
Isn't it just the factor that all the terms contrive to
Shape to some kind of formulation, however clumsy?
Wouldn't success in this way be a relative sort of objective?
Not as a matter of pride, and certainly not of money,
But simply all by itself, being the common factor?
Well, neither is wholly true nor wholly false: I assert
Over the black and the white the exact ascendance of greyness.
That is something I fear they don't understand in New Orleans
Where questions of fact with the guns hang silently over the fireplace
And motive is whispered in fields or assassinated in ballrooms,
And pride is assigned to success, and weakness of course to failure
(Try telling Uncle Ernest to take a pride in failure!).
Can you in honesty say that this disturbs and dismays you?
Mother, I ask you again: what do you think you are losing?
Is it my loss you fear, or might it be *my* losing?
If it were *that* I should smile, for it seems a fitting emotion
For one who has vowed to defy such a majestic opponent.
But, as I say, I find emotion a difficult subject.
That is of course my weakness, but weakness may lead to success,
For only a firm resolve and a singleness of purpose
Keep us applied to the matter in hand where feeling is stranger
And the mind runs even and smooth, oiled in a beautiful silence.
    Here in England, chess takes its proper place as a pastime.
It is not such a solemn affair, and yet, to be sure, it is serious:
Mother, I fear you could not understand the way it is taken,
Though sometimes when you sit at the piano I think you must know,
But if you know, you are silent, and silent most in talking:
There are some desperate silences when you're engaged in talking!
Hell. This looks like being another one of those letters
In which I say too much, – which I never get round to sending.
It's not so much a case of distance lending enchantment,
Licence to speak one's mind while the magic spell's unbroken;
Simply that such a perspective inclines one to see things clearly.
So must all travellers feel getting down at the end of their journey.

For me, as you know, the event had a strange and significant
        meaning,
Liverpool sighted in patchy fog, June the twenty-first,
The *Arabia* docking at noon on the eve of my coming-of-age.
Newspapermen were not slow, I'm afraid, to remark on the date:
Did my parents object before, and was that the only reason
Why previously I had seemed unwilling to make the journey?
Facts, facts. What could I say? *Did* you give your consent?
I have to admit to myself that I really can't remember.
To the newspapermen I admitted the name of my hotel only,
Tired as I was and endlessly probed by their fatuous questions:
How many shirts did I have? Would I visit the opera?
That seventeenth move in my game in November with Paulsen,
Did I remember? Of course. The sacrifice of the queen.
I offered a clear and simple exchange of my queen for his bishop.
Paulsen was sure at the outset that it was a trap, cunning but
Obvious in a way, not one to easily fall for.
'Paulsen had worked out the combinations for six moves ahead, sir,
Six moves ahead! Taking an hour, and all the spectators
Excited and restless. An hour of thinking, and still couldn't see it.
Did he think you were mad, sir? He sat and he sat and he wondered
And took your queen. And the crowd gasped! And you said nothing.
Paulsen was forced to capitulate after eleven moves,
Eleven incredible moves ahead. Can you say, Mr Morphy,
What went on in your mind? Did you know? Had you worked it all
        out?
Or was it simply a stroke of luck, a leap in the darkness?'
    Silly to say that there's nothing to say, but it's true, there isn't.
All of us live in the dark, and many decline to leap
And so I knew that Paulsen would find it a deal of trouble.
Would it make news? I'd no idea, but I hoped it wouldn't.
News isn't really new but a long continuing process,
Daily refinement of what the readers have learned to expect.
Mine I have kept to the last, though you won't be thrilled to hear it.
Perhaps it won't absolutely displease you. It fills the paper,
And what is there else to do but to come to the end of the page,
The period which our pen proposes, or else turn over
To find that the sick white blank of the other side awaits us?
For pride is assigned to success, and weakness of course to failure,

And silence (how can we doubt it?) has nothing to do with feeling.
No, mother, I sign off here, and say: I have written to Staunton,
Written again to Staunton in the friendliest possible terms.
Can you in honesty say that this disturbs and dismays you?
How can it do that? No, I think you must wish me success,
But don't imagine it's pride that leads me on to the conquest.
No one who saw me now could ever think that it was.

        ✻   ✻   ✻

No letters from home as yet, from you, or Helen, or Ernest,
But then there's nothing from Charles, and he would certainly write,
So I don't say this to rebuke but to damn the Atlantic packet
And to show how sick I am of the praise and the pearls and the parties.
Last night I heard Miss Louisa Pyne at the Philharmonic
In a pretty duet from the *Freischütz* before the Queen and Prince
     Consort:
Such idleness, such automatic applause before such beauty!
The English are superb, superb in their lack of thinking.
Quite early in the evening the gas went low and nearly
Disturbed the spectators' sleep with a fear of being left in the darkness.
Small drama, I know, but a real one, this fear of being left in the
     darkness,
Real like the fear of silence, the fear of the empty page.
To date I have written two, no three, plain letters to Staunton,
Three plain letters of challenge and always the same:
I will play you, he says, in September, in September or else in October.
I need just a few more weeks to brush up my openings and endings.
I will play you, he says, in October, in October or else in November.
    The curtain is rising for ever and the stage is always empty,
The rooms are impeccably dusted, the rooms with the lilies and roses,
The rooms that look out on the front, the rooms above Piccadilly,
The rooms in the feminine capital, the rooms of the Second Empire
(All good Americans when they die end up in Paris!),
The rooms all over Europe whose doors are incessantly opening,
Inviting the guest to flip open the well-filled silver inkwell,
To dip and relate with unaccustomed pen his travels.
All over Europe from room to room and always the same:
The doors are opening freely and the curtain is rising,
The sofas and chairs are placed just so, and the roses and lilies,

All the forwarded messages, cables and invitations,
And the little escritoire – there, in the right-hand corner!
Inviting the guest to record a transient name on the blotter,
Faint and reversed as the dreams he will dream on the single pillow.
Where is the action? Where is the speech and magnificent lighting?
Knuckles are still in repose at the end of my cuffs like tree-roots,
Springs of expensive clocks dilate in their glittering coils,
Visitors come and go on matters of no importance
And the curtain is rising for ever and the stage is always empty.

       ✻   ✻   ✻

That was a month ago already, and the letter's still with me.
Letters not sent assume a life of their own like monsters:
A sudden slow stare right into the gilt frame of the spirit
When only the eyes are seen but you know they belong to a stranger
And the memory can't be dispelled; it horribly lingers for ever.
The mouth is gaping open, the sickening flap unsealed.
You can't escape that singular moment of recognition:
Turn on the polished heel, fold back the unfolded paper,
But ever the haunting vision hovers over your shoulder,
Something that you created and will not let you ignore it,
A poor disfigured creature full of immortal longings,
A sort of ideal maimed by the uncontrolling hand,
A life that only endures as a vestige of what was intended.
Are we the same as we were, and will that be always the same?
My letter begins with rebukes, but that was a month ago,
A sloughed-off self in a limbo of lonely introspection.
That was already a month ago, and the letter's still with me.
I found it just now in a drawer with my socks in the hotel bedroom
And thought about what you had said of the praise and the girls and
      the parties,
And all my anger was gone when I came to the matter in hand.
At a distance all quarrels diminish and tend to resolve themselves into
A hard plain conglomeration of fact like a lawsuit.
But what is the law to say of the distance of space and time?
The law has nothing to do with time, as not of its making.
The law has nothing to do with space, for that it may break.
I felt today the first futility of the challenge
And all the sad impurities of life rose up together

As if to seize for themselves a prize that was not awarded,
And whiskered faces cheered, and no one was any the wiser.
   Can you imagine an afternoon in the north of England
In a flat damp August, sticky enough, but more dirty than sticky,
Walking across the Queen's College Birmingham's brown narrow
      lawns?
On one side your true representative of modern American manners,
On the other the large *doyen* of large British Chess, Mr Staunton,
And as umpire Lord Lyttelton trotting, perspiring a little,
Blotting his face with a large chequered kerchief covered with pawns?
No one would try to keep the peace between two such as
Staunton and I seemed to be on that gloomy and brief occasion,
Only a man who had nothing to offer, and he had nothing.
'Howard?' he kept on saying, in a tone of interrogation
As close as it could get to an undemanding statement:
'Howard?' But Staunton in the blandest possible manner,
Pausing only to lift a fading rose with one finger,
Talked without saying a thing, talked without making an answer,
Talked in a general way, smiled and was utterly charming.
'I will play you,' he said, 'in September, in September or else in
      October:
I need just a few more weeks to be clear of my other affairs,
Affairs of the greatest importance I'm sure you understand.
What a delightful game! Delightful and scientific!
Scientific and moral, too, most moral of hobbies!'
   So it went on, and he forced me to feel the shame of persistence,
The squirming abject shame of inflicting myself upon him,
Taking his time and trying to hold him down to a promise;
Forced upon me the role of callow importuner
Seizing my chance to exploit a gentleman's casual interest,
Working with careful words and casual professional phrases
To lure him to some intense and somehow dangerous tourney;
Forced upon me the rôle of the eager smooth-talking gambler,
Cheeky at roadside inn or on Mississippi steamer;
Forced me to nod insanely at his procrastination:
'I will play you,' he said, 'in October, in October or else in November.'
What could I say? I felt I had somehow yielded a move for
Though in England chess takes its proper place as a pastime,
Though it is not such a solemn affair, it has its own logic

And none in its deadly motions more practised than Howard
    Staunton,
Motions of serpentine skill and brazen prevarication,
Motions that know how they can afford to be lazily charming.
Lyttelton did his best, but his best was quite sadly useless:
November is merely a dream. The summer will fly like a winner,
Turf be untrodden, the crowds dispersed to their occupations.
Nothing can season the shocking taste of his blank refusal,
Nothing awaken him from his dream of victorious inaction,
Nothing disturb the unruffled surface of condescension,
The idle furloughs and barracks of a giant reputation,
The imperious posture of one who's unwilling to risk defeat.
I know it. And yet I hope. Hope against hope that sometime
The proud façade will crack, and light flood into the building.
But the curtain is rising for ever and the stage is always empty.

        ❊   ❊   ❊

To have no desires; worse, to have a desire for desires,
Is the death of the soul in its terrible grip of desiring to please.
Not the ideal, the burning ambition or even a hunger
For the trivial flush of content, the certain fact of fulfilment,
Simply the struggle to act one's part with the secret knowledge
That *this* is how it must be and nobody else may gainsay you.
How can I keep some sense of faith in my own objectives?
No one to trust, no one, and least of all the dragon
Roaring slightly again with his still-smouldering breath,
Saying at first he would only play in consultation,
Prowling about the tournament hall like a proud head-waiter,
Ready to offer advice to anyone he could rally,
Bland as a fighting bishop blessing the last battalion,
Lyttelton in despair, the Birmingham hotels full.
Now he announces his entry as quietly as he is able!
Staunton's decided to enter now that the lists are complete!
What's the idea? Does he want to storm his way through the talent,
Blaming a lucky accident if I manage to stop him,
Hoping I'll fall by chance to the Reverend Henry Salmon,
Hoping one way or another we'll never actually meet?
Credit will have to be given for such an adroit reversal
Coolly and casually made when nobody seemed to be looking!

One thing is wrong with his plan, though: I shan't be there in
    person.
I wanted a private match, and the tournament doesn't amuse me.
Tomorrow I have proposed eight games without sight of the pieces,
Eight games together on Wednesday, sitting away from the tables.
Avery, Kipping and Wills, Rhodes, Carr and Dr Freeman
All have agreed with indecent haste to the blind encounter.
Lyttelton too will play, and the Reverend Henry Salmon.
Then I shall leave for Paris to see what *they* have to offer.
Anderssen will be there and others, perhaps, with manners.
Nothing is left for me here, at least till Birmingham's over.

                        ❊   ❊   ❊

The curtain is rising still and the stage is always empty.
Why must we have a will when we don't know how to direct it?
Why must we have above all this dreadful desire for desires?
Where does the impulse come from? Do we acquire it, I wonder?
Or is it a secret alloy in the chain of bleeding that binds us
Fast to our foul perpetual history? Unwilling victims!
That I suppose was what in the first place moved me to study
How men have so arranged their affairs to make some kind of sense:
Power to do what the law allows is the only freedom.
Wriggling cells succumb to these ordered inventions of man, but
What is the law to say of the struggle of space and time?
The law has nothing to do with time, as not of its making.
The law has nothing to do with space, for that it may break.
Only the rules it energizes, the rules and the fictions,
And I feel your heart across the sea making do with fictions,
For I sacrificed your strength for the sake of a wretched stalemate.
Some sort of brilliant sacrifice lies behind every challenge,
But to offer Andromeda up as a tasty bait for the dragon
And the dragon to turn up his nose: I can hardly bear to think it.

    At Birmingham, Staunton was out in the second round. Retiring
To Richmond to lick his wounds, he used his column to bait me.
It's clear we shall never play, and I will be home by Christmas.
And the *Illustrated London News* and the *New Orleans Delta*,
Even the *Birmingham Post*, will have to make do with fictions,
The fictions of law, the fictions of rules, the fictions of papers,
And the fictions of black and white, the thirty-two little fictions

Which have nothing to do with the heart, for that they may break
And what they break stands apart and watches in space and time
And I have failed you, mother, and cannot bear your look.
I have failed to kill the dragon, though Europe bows down before me.
I have failed to fulfil your strength, though Anderssen smiled in defeat
And deafened Paris suspected another revolution!
I have failed in the field of success, and my pride must give place to my
    weakness,
The weakness of wishing too much to engage in the pure world of
    mind,
Flickering light beyond the frowning behind the blindfold,
World where the thought rides on blood, instinctive in the darkness.
And what has the law to say of this fear of being left in the darkness?
What has the law to say of a son and his broken heart?

3   STAUNTON EPILOGIZES (SPRING, 1865)

The desk is piled. Untired and regular
As mercury the level in trunk and stem
Rises, the old engagement, the old trumpets.
No question of anything different ever happening!
Those ducks on the lawn: every May they come
From their slowly moving home to a green slumber,
Heads tucked, dozing obliquely in marital content
Too far for snappishness or love's mirror-tricks
But close enough to have the air of posing
Like frugal boulders in that Kyoto garden
Perry reported, or perhaps a cannon at billiards.
All Nature mating with a *pion coiffé*!
Wasteful, prolific of rejected seeds
So one, the most unlikely, should win through.
And early roses just the same: trustful!
    There will be frost, and you are far from here.
There will be frost, and nothing is the same.
Nothing can last, and everything is different.
I miss you! There's no one else to gather roses
And float them in silver dishes on the table.
Shutters are flapping. The hall is like a ballroom

Polka'd with dust. Strange: you learned your freedom
From your dependence, and that long beautiful boredom
Rose armed from the gradual wreck of a girlhood frolic.
Much too young to be shut up in a tower!
You said I kept away too long from you
And so men do, I think, but it's not right:
The shoots burst from the fragile trellis, all
The buds in wild profusion lean in the air,
Crossed, straggling, heavy, burdened down.
All of us bear our load, but the free spirit
Never forgives the bondage of its peers.
We have no time, alas, for heroes now:
Beneath snug tailoring its fiery hair
And plated muscles of a Fuseli angel
Strain to express a quiddity. And you,
Your head full of such antique pictures. My fault.
I should have seen your meaning better, dear.
I should have taken greater care of you.
You and your perfect body were my text
And all its cruces hidden. Now it's too late.
　　A life of caring for the insights of
Another man! I sometimes felt, with Pope
And the finest of the early editors,
That the real task lay not in tidying-up
Errors and riddles of the leaden case
But in the niceties of taste and skill,
The signposts to the choicest passages,
Reader to reader. Likewise the pleasure lay
In the approval not the scorn of moves,
And I could well have wished a silent mark
Of exclamation to adorn the Swan
Many and many a time. What can one say?
When I approved, you glowed, or seemed to glow.
Perhaps unspoken pleasure in your graces
Seemed like a deafness where in truth it was
A simple echo of your quietness.
I was there. I heard. And in the end I lost.
　　At least I have preserved ascendancy
In the science. Anderssen is broken and

They tell me Morphy's mad now: shouts in the street
And follows no profession. Sues his brother
For the father's fortune. Certainly won't play chess.
Well, well. One might have guessed it, but the cause
Is none too clear. What was the truth of the matter?
Did some kind tutelary spirit lean
From the rococo clouds with ready crown,
Strike Harrwitz down and give him Anderssen,
Whose play afforded shocking evidence
Of being no longer the victor's of '51?
Did we resent his luck and nerve? For my part
I had no particular feelings, retired as I was
From practical chess. How could I risk the stakes
So rashly offered by my generous friends?
I might have played a game or two, *sans façon*.
I even steeled myself to Birmingham
And entered with a show of chivalry:
Morphy refused to play! There one has it.
The tender bloom, forced under glass, must wilt
On contact with the ordinary air.
That *you* would understand, I think, my dear!
Who gave me at the time one long cool stare.
Yet those who would perform *kotoo* before the boy
(And rush to do the same before whoever's
The times' top-sawyer) can't be satisfied
To give him endless *kudos* among themselves
Without the blowing of a penny-trumpet
To call to homage all the sentient world!
Grant the achievement, and the wish to play
David to Europe's grave Goliaths, yet
It was not such a salient episode.
There was a basic failure of the will,
A trust to risk, exploiting combinations.
Eight blindfold games, remembering all the moves?
A piece of rhetoric, the science served
To better purpose by my little handbook,
Bilguer and der Laza much improved,
And read in clubs and cafés everywhere.
    I still have that, and much besides. Or do I?

148

At night after some bruxist escapade,
Waking in sweat, I pad down to this study
And stare at the piled desk and all these papers
To which the attached ink is a history
Of a long hunger and fatal miscalculation.
I could be Claudius at prayer! But no,
That's silly. Even a villain has some presence.
Once proud of my pride in what I had achieved
Now I have only the abject achievement.
Once in love with the harmony of our orbits
Now I feel only the fierce lack at the centre.
I've risked nothing and everything is lost!
Ah, well. The deadly promptness of the spring
Becomes a kind of welcome remedy.
Its scenery is sufficient. It obeys
The rules. Those ducks, the ostentatious roses,
Even the diligent editor of Shakespeare,
All move in free compulsion to one end
Which though unknown is wholly necessary
And has some joys, I think. Or sometimes does.

JOHN FULLER

Opponent

My father would never be defeated.

Whenever the game got hot, and there was
a chance of somebody else winning,
he'd leave the table and take his little
portable set and study all the possible moves
sitting in the damp blue toilet off the hall
until the seat was warm right through to the china.

At other times, when his heavy immobile
white hand hovered too long over the ivory pieces,
I wanted to impale it with a kitchen skewer
like a slab of meat; but one thing stopped me –
my conviction that the blood would be black.

We used to have tournaments: we used names
my grandfather invented: my captain was
a Red Indian called Big Bottom, my father's a Chinaman,
Wun Hung Lo: we had teams of three, and nine games.

Once in Norway when I had captured his Queen,
he knew the game was up; but being the man he was,
he simply resigned, much too early, to make sure that
it was impossible for anyone else to win.

For three years now, we've been sending our moves
by postcard; it takes four days each way.
But one thing is missing: neither of us can enjoy
at such distance, the polished squares of mutual
hatred that always kept the game for us horribly alive.

GAVIN BANTOCK

Chess Master

A strange place to play that last game,
Out there on the wind crazed island.
   Arthritic trees ringed us
In while the old man flung my same
Manoeuvres into the baize lined
   Box. 'I've played,' he burred as

My bishops wandered off on their
Obvious tangents, 'with the best,
   Laddie.' He did not mind
The rain which had started to clear
A growling sky nor that the waste
   Lay down under a wind

Which worried the hairs on his hand
And unseated my quixotic
   Knights. I talked of getting
Back before dark to the mainland
And felt the Channel chaotic
   Once again, buffeting

My fear. 'I've played with the best, son,'
He muttered, watching me nudge out
   A reluctant rook. 'You
Could in the old times.' And yet one
Day, he'd always known, he would sit
   Down to that game. A few

Days later, I heard he had died
And the wind in the gutters kept
   Heckling my peace, like the
Capsized king rolling on our board,
Back, forth, as if it had not stopped
   And could not die away.

Ian Caws

On Her Taking my Queen at Chess

I opened King's knight pawn to King's knight three
And so King's bishop up to King's knight two
Then I moved King's knight to King's bishop three:
She preferred black, I thought so too
My first move might reveal my strategy!

So to mislead I did not castle yet
But chased one of her knights about
Which was unsupported, and spread my net
On her Queen's side, and drew my own Queen out,
Alas, it is so easy to forget
What chess is basically all about:

Men tend to think in a prosaic way,
Identify the ends and find the means,
And chess to them is somewhat like a play
With all the plotting done behind the scenes,
But chess to women is like everyday
Only even more so, and Kings and Queens
Are you and me, in an odd sort of way.
(They think of knights as horses though, it seems.)

I thought I had been circumspect, but no:
My Queen provoked the utmost jealousy,
It may just be hormonal, I don't know
It may be simply married chastity,
But she was doomed, and I to let her go
She was surrounded by the enemy
Who most ingeniously struck her low.

It was an almost human sacrifice
And nearly all the quality were there,
Their Queen had triumphed, but at what a price
The King's side of the chessboard was quite bare!

I saw my moves and knew they would suffice
And played and got checkmate, but did she care?
'Your Queen!' she said, which wasn't very nice,
'I got your Queen that time' she said, 'so THERE!'

SIMON LOWY

Bibliography and Acknowledgements

The following is a list of the books used as sources for poems and excerpts included in this anthology. Place of publication is the United Kingdom unless otherwise stated.

1 WORKS BY INDIVIDUAL AUTHORS

Conrad Aiken, *Selected Poems*, New York, 1961. Extract from 'Preludes for Memnon, LVI' from *Selected Poems* by Conrad Aiken. Copyright © by Conrad Aiken. Reprinted by permission of Oxford University Press, Inc.

W. H. Auden, *About the House*, 1966. Extract from 'Symmetries and Asymmetries' reprinted by permission of Faber and Faber Ltd and Random House, Inc.

Gavin Bantock, *Dragons*, 1979. 'Opponent' reprinted by permission of Anvil Press Poetry Ltd.

Francis Beaumont and John Fletcher, *The Works of Francis Beaumont and John Fletcher*, vol. VI, ed. A. R. Waller, 1908.

Patricia Beer, *Loss of the Magyar*, 1959. 'Checkmate' reprinted by permission of Patricia Beer.

John Berryman, *Selected Poems 1938–1968*, 1972. 'The Moon and the Night and the Men' reprinted by permission of Faber and Faber Ltd and Farrar, Straus & Giroux, Inc.

Richard Burton, *The Book of the Thousand Nights and a Night*, 1885.

Jack Carey, *Words and Mirrors*, 1976. 'Games' reprinted by permission of the author.

Ian Caws, *Boy with a Kite*, 1981. 'Chess Master' reprinted by permission of Ian Caws and Sidgwick & Jackson Ltd.

Geoffrey Chaucer, *The Works of Geoffrey Chaucer*, ed. F. N. Robinson, 1957.

Abraham Cowley, *Poems*, ed. A. R. Waller, 1905.

Marcus Cumberlege, *Firelines*, 1977. 'Lord Dunsany' reprinted by permission of Anvil Press Poetry Ltd.

Edward Fitzgerald, *Rubáiyát of Omar Khayyám* (1st edn.), 1859.

John Fuller, *Lies and Secrets*, 1978. 'The Most Difficult Position' reprinted by permission of Secker and Warburg Ltd.

Oliver Goldsmith, *The Poems of Goldsmith*, 1880.

Peter Jay, *Shifting Frontiers*, 1980. 'A Game of Chess' and 'Life of the Pawn' reprinted by permission of Carcanet Press Ltd.

Elizabeth Jennings, *Collected Poems 1967*, 1967. 'A Game of Chess' reprinted by permission of Macmillan, London and Basingstoke.

Sir William Jones, *Poems*, 1772.

Lotte Kramer, *Family Arrivals*, 1981. 'Chess' reprinted by permission of the author and Poet & Printer.

Richard Lovelace, *The Poems of Richard Lovelace*, ed. C. H. Wilkinson, 1930.

Robert Lowell, *Imitations*, 1962; *History*, 1973. 'The Chess Player' and 'The Winner' reprinted by permission of Faber and Faber Ltd and Farrar, Straus & Giroux, Inc.

Simon Lowy, *Melusine & the Nigredo*, 1979. 'On Her Taking my Queen at Chess' reprinted by permission of Carcanet Press Ltd.

John Lydgate, *Reson and Sensuallyte*, ed. Ernst Sieper, Early English Text Society Extra Series, 84, 89, 1901–1903; *Troy Book*, ed. Henry Bergen, Early English Text Society 97, 103, 106, 126, 1906–1935.

Louis MacNeice, *Collected Poems*, 1966. 'Chess' and 'Another Cold May' reprinted by permission of Faber and Faber Ltd.

John Masefield, *Collected Poems*, 1923. Extract from 'The Widow in the Bye Street' reprinted by permission of The Society of Authors as the literary representatives of the Estate of John Masefield, and Macmillan Publishing Co., Inc.

Thomas Middleton, *Women Beware Women*, ed. J. R. Mulryne, 1975; *A Game at Chess*, ed. J. W. Harper, 1966.

R. H. Morrison, *Opus 4*, Melbourne, 1971; *The Secret Greenness and other Poems*, Melbourne, 1978. 'Chess Men' and 'Checkmate' reprinted by permission of the author and The Hawthorn Press.

Howard Nemerov, *The Next Room of the Dream*, Chicago, 1962. 'Idea' reprinted by permission of the author.

Ezra Pound, *Collected Shorter Poems*, 1952. 'The Game of Chess' reprinted by permission of Faber and Faber Ltd. Ezra Pound, *Personae*. Copyright 1926 by Ezra Pound. Reprinted by permission of New Directions, New York.

Edwin Arlington Robinson, *Collected Poems*, New York, 1937. 'Atherton's Gambit' from *The Town Down the River* by Edwin Arlington Robinson. Copyright 1910 by Charles Scribner's Sons; copyright renewed. Reprinted by permission of Macmillan Publishing Co., Inc.

John Skelton, *Poems*, selected and edited by Robert S. Kinsman, 1969.

The Romance of Guy of Warwick, ed. Julius Zupitsa, Early English Text Society Extra Series, 25–26, 1875–1876.

Lord Alfred Tennyson, *Poetical Works*, Oxford Standard Authors, 1953.

R. S. Thomas, *Frequencies*, 1978. 'Play' reprinted by permission of Macmillan, London and Basingstoke.

Charles Tomlinson, F.R.S., *Chess, a poem in four cantos together with minor poems and aphorisms*, 1891.

Andrew Waterman, *Over the Wall*, 1980. 'The Game's the Thing' and 'Playing Through Old Games of Chess' reprinted by permission of Carcanet Press Ltd.

W. B. Yeats, *The Variorum Edition of the Poems of W. B. Yeats*, eds. Peter Allt and Russell K. Alspach, New York, 1957. Extract from *Time and the Witch Vivien* reprinted by permission of Macmillan Publishing Co., Inc., M. B. Yeats, Anne Yeats and Macmillan London Ltd.

A Book of Australian and New Zealand Verse, eds. Walter Murdoch and Alan Mulgan, 1950, for 'Chess' by John Thompson, reprinted by permission of Patricia Thompson.

Chess: A Compilation of all the Anecdotes and Quotations that could be found relative to the Game of Chess, Richard Twiss, 1787, for the anonymous lines entitled by the present editor 'The Man that Hath No Love of Chess'.

Chess Pieces, ed. Norman Knight, 1949, for translation by 'G.B.' from Vida's *Scacchia Ludus*, and 'A Pawn's a Pawn for A' That' by W. Cook Spens, originally published in *The Glasgow Herald*, 1883.

Der Mittelenglische Versroman über Richard Löwenherz (Richard Cuer de Lyon), ed. K. Brunner, Wien-Leipzig, 1913, for lines excerpted by the present editor as 'King Richard'.

Oxford Book of Irish Verse, eds. D. McDonagh and L. Robinson, 1950, for 'Chesspieces' by Joseph Campbell, reprinted by permission of Simon Campbell.

Oxford Book of Victorian Verse, chosen by Arthur Quiller-Couch, for 'The Chess Board' by E. R. Bulwer Lytton, Earl of Lytton.

Religious Lyrics of the Fifteenth Century, ed. Carleton Brown, 1939, for the anonymous 'Good Rule is Out of Remembrance' (no. 172), from which are excerpted the lines entitled by the present editor 'Both Check and Mate'.

The Chess Lovers' Calendar for 1911 for the anonymous poem entitled by the present editor 'The Game of the Pawn and the Queen'.

The Early English Carols, ed. Richard Leighton Greene, 1935, for the anonymous 'Strife in the House' (no. 408) from which are excerpted the lines entitled by the present editor 'Checkmate'.

The Golden Year, Poetry Society of America Anthology (1919–1960), eds. Melville Cane, John Farrar and Louisa Townsend Nicholl, New York, 1960, for 'Duel in the Park' by Lisa Grenelle.

The Phoenix Nest (1593), facsimile publication by The Scolar Press (1973), for 'The Chess Play' by Nicholas Breton.

Tottel's Miscellany (1557), facsimile publication ed. Hyder Edward Rollins, 1966, for 'To the Lady that Scorned her Lover' by Henry Howard, Earl of Surrey.

3

For poems previously unpublished in book form we thank the following: Gerard Benson for 'Lost and Found' and 'Chess Piece' (under the pseudonym Jedediah Barrow); John Campbell-Kease for 'Shah Mat'; Barry Cole for 'A Game of Chess'; John Holmstrom for 'Check'; David Jenkins for 'The Chess Lesson'; Carol Rumens for 'Chess Players', published in *Stand* vol. 20, no. 1, 1978 and 'A Poem for Chessmen at a Congress', published in *The London Review of Books*, vol. 3, no. 11, 1981; Joy Rutherford for 'Pawn'; Pauline Stainer for 'Medieval Chess King'; J. P. Ward for 'Carved Pieces' and J. A.

Wareing for 'Chess'. Lord Dunsany's poems – 'Epitaph for Capablanca', published in *Chess*, 1943 and 'The Sea and Chess', written for the Hastings Chess Congress, 1951 – are reprinted by kind permission of Curtis Brown Ltd, on behalf of John Child-Villiers and Valentine Lamb as literary executors of Lord Dunsany.

Every effort has been made to trace the copyright holders of Lisa Grenelle's poem 'Duel in the Park', but this has proved impossible.

Index of Poets